Distributed Leadership in Schools

GW00777494

Building on best practices and lessons learned, *Distributed Leadership in Schools* shows educators how to design and implement distributed leadership to effectively address challenges in their schools. Grounded in case studies and full of practical tools, this book lays out a framework for building strategic, collaborative, and instructionally focused teams. Supported by voices of practitioners and based upon original research, this comprehensive resource shares concrete strategies, tips, and tools for creating teams that are skilled at using data to plan and monitor their work, and successful in facilitating change to improve student learning. This innovative method will aid leader development and facilitate reflection, and will reshape leadership practice in a way that benefits teachers, leaders, schools, and students.

John A. DeFlaminis is Executive Director of the Penn Center for Educational Leadership, Director of the Distributed Leadership Program, and adjunct Professor in the Graduate School of Education at the University of Pennsylvania, USA.

Mustafa Abdul-Jabbar has served as a teacher, school administrator, director of diversity initiatives for schools, and education researcher.

Eric Yoak has served as a teacher, school principal, school district administrator, and in university-based roles aimed at supporting leadership development research and practice. He currently works as a school administrator in a large urban district and teaches courses in leadership and research methods.

Other Eye On Education Books Available from Routledge
(www.routledge.com/eyeoneducation)

Strategies for Developing and Supporting School Leaders: Stepping Stones to Great Leadership
Karen L. Sanzo

Crafting the Feedback Teachers Need and Deserve: A Guide for Leaders
Thomas Van Soelen

Becoming a Social Justice Leader: Using Head, Heart, and Hands to Dismantle Oppression
Phil Hunsberger, Billie Mayo, and Anthony Neal

Formative Assessment Leadership: Identify, Plan, Apply, Assess, Refine
Karen L. Sanzo, Steve Myran, and John Caggiano

The Leader's Guide to Working with Underperforming Teachers: Overcoming Marginal Teaching and Getting Results
Sally J. Zepeda

Five Critical Leadership Practices: The Secret to High-Performing Schools
Ruth C. Ash and Pat H. Hodge

Mentoring is a Verb: Strategies for Improving College and Career Readiness
Russ Olwell

How to Make Data Work: A Guide for Educational Leaders
Jenny Grant Rankin

Hiring the Best Staff for Your School: How to Use Narrative to Improve Your Recruiting Process
Rick Jetter

What Connected Educators Do Differently
Todd Whitaker, Jeffrey Zoul, and Jimmy Casas

Job-Embedded Professional Development: Support, Collaboration, and Learning in Schools
Sally J. Zepeda

Distributed Leadership in Schools

A Practical Guide for Learning
and Improvement

John A. DeFlaminis, Mustafa
Abdul-Jabbar, and Eric Yoak

Routledge
Taylor & Francis Group

NEW YORK AND LONDON

First published 2016
by Routledge
711 Third Avenue, New York, NY 10017

and by Routledge
2 Park Square, Milton Park, Abingdon, Oxon, OX14 4RN

Routledge is an imprint of the Taylor & Francis Group, an informa business

Library of Congress Cataloging in Publication Data
A catalog record for this book has been requested

ISBN: 978-1-138-84599-2 (hbk)
ISBN: 978-1-138-84600-5 (pbk)
ISBN: 978-1-315-72775-2(ebk)

Typeset in Optima
by Swales & Willis Ltd, Exeter, Devon, UK

Printed and bound in the United States of America by Publishers Graphics,
LLC on sustainably sourced paper.

Contents

Contents

Meet the Authors

John A. DeFlaminis, Ph.D.

Dr. DeFlaminis is the Executive Director of the Penn Center for Educational Leadership (PCEL) at the University of Pennsylvania's Graduate School of Education. He also leads the Distributed Leadership Program, which he developed when he came to Penn in 2004. This program has had three extensive implementations (including an Annenberg Grant) totaling over $10 million to support new principals struggling in poor urban schools, by surrounding them with extensively trained teacher leaders. He has served as adjunct Professor of Education at Penn, and has taught and advised doctoral students in the Mid-Career Doctoral and the Aspiring Principals Program.

Throughout his career, his teaching has ranged from elementary through university. He completed his Ph.D. at the University of Oregon's Center for Educational Policy and Management, concentrating on administration and organizational psychology. His research there focused on team teaching and leadership development. Next, he taught at the University of Louisville while codeveloping a doctoral program for school leaders, and also writing/administering several federally and state-funded grants targeting leadership development and delivery of training to field administrators.

Prior to joining Penn's Graduate School of Education, Dr. DeFlaminis was superintendent of the Radnor Township School District for seventeen years, leading the direction and development of strategic, capital improvement, staff development, curriculum development, and technology plans.

He also developed extensive evaluation processes at all levels, encompassing administrative and teacher-performance appraisal systems, and extensive program evaluations in six major areas, including management services. His priorities covered the development and implementation of an internationally benchmarked, standards-based system in all curricular areas with K-12 performance assessments.

Dr. DeFlaminis has consulted nationally and internationally with the U.S. Department of Education, several State Departments of education, rural and urban school districts, administrative organizations, private business organizations, and the Kettering Foundation. His workshops, articles, and keynote speeches have often addressed key management processes, such as motivation, leadership, and change. He has also led several statewide organizations and been a board member in others, including the Pennsylvania Association of School Administrators, the Pennsylvania Educational Research Association, and the Radnor Educational Foundation.

Mustafa Abdul-Jabbar, Ed.D.

Dr. Abdul-Jabbar has served as a teacher, school administrator, director of diversity initiatives for schools, and an education researcher. He has an avid interest in understanding how education policy is best designed and implemented at all levels of governance. His specific expertise is in working with teachers and administrators, leadership teams, and leadership preparation programs, most recently with the Penn Center for Educational Leadership (PCEL), where he worked with the Archdiocese of Philadelphia to develop and implement a distributed leadership approach in their schools. This included professional development and training, program evaluation, and coaching support for school leadership teams.

Dr. Abdul-Jabbar received his doctorate in educational leadership from the University of Pennsylvania, where he served as a research fellow with the Office of Academic Innovation. His work there involved the strategic utilization of social media, increasing student access to learning through massive open online courses (MOOCs), developing instructional/informational webinars, staging virtual events, and hosting educational innovation competitions at the university. He expects his juris doctor degree from Harvard Law School in 2016.

Eric Yoak, Ed.D.

Dr. Yoak's work as an educator is driven by his belief in the transformative power of education and his awareness of the great inequities that persist in our schools and school systems. He has served as a teacher, school principal, school district administrator, and in university-based roles in research and policy.

Dr. Yoak's areas of expertise include school leadership, adult learning and professional development, organizational design, and education policy. His research on adult learning in the context of school-based professional development elucidates the processes of individual growth and their relationship to schoolwide change in instructional practices and organizational culture.

Most notably, this has been informed by his relationship with the Distributed Leadership Program at the Penn Center for Educational Leadership (PCEL), where he designed and implemented evaluative research, action research, and professional development seminars for school-based teams of administrators and teacher leaders.

Foreword

Distributed leadership, or a distributed perspective on leadership, has garnered considerable attention over the past fifteen years. Numerous researchers, policymakers, and practitioners are taking a distributed perspective on school leadership and management. But distributed leadership has come to mean many things to many people; it is often used interchangeably with other concepts such as "democratic leadership" and "shared leadership." Further, some write as though distributed leadership is about little more than an acknowledgment that the work of leadership and management extends beyond the school principal, making one wonder at times if distributed leadership is just another case of old wine in new bottles. Such loose usage is problematic, and potentially undermines the potency of the notion of distributed leadership.

This book is a welcome departure. John DeFlaminis and his colleagues, in the chapters that follow, carefully "operationalize" (their word) distributed leadership by describing and analyzing the Annenberg Distributed Leadership Project. The Annenberg Distributed Leadership Project is one of the most ambitious efforts (perhaps the most ambitious) to date, to put a distributed leadership perspective into practice in the professional development of school leaders. By describing their efforts to design a program of professional development for teams of leaders from schools, and implement that program into schools, the authors offer a rich, theoretically anchored, and practice-focused account of distributed leadership in practice. As such, the book offers the most comprehensive guide to implementing distributed leadership in professional development. But it does more. Because the program of professional development also offered complementary support in schools for the professional development program—such as leadership coaching for leadership teams—the book provides insights into the real work and challenges of doing distributed leadership in schools. The authors have a deep appreciation for the practice of leading and managing. As a result, the account of implementing distributed leadership provided here will ring true to practitioners on the ground.

While this is *the* book on distributed leadership for practicing system and school leaders (in part a function of the authors' extensive experience as practicing school-building and school-system leaders), it is much more than a guide for practitioners. The book is also theoretically rich, with the authors carefully motivating and anchoring their design decisions for their professional development program and school support in the theoretical literature. As such, the book documents one of the most thoughtful and theoretically authentic efforts at putting a distributed perspective into practice in developing and supporting teams of leaders from schools. Too often, researchers dumb down theoretical ideas for practitioners and policymakers. Or, policymakers and practitioners, in an effort to make theory workable and usable, dumb it down for those they work with: distributed leadership lite. And these translations often undermine the potency of ideas. These authors avoid such common pitfalls, working faithfully with the theoretical ideas in the design and deployment of the Annenberg Distributed Leadership Project. As a result, the book provides the most compelling account of attempting to authentically translate a set of ideas about distributed leadership into a fleshed-out program of development and support for schools wanting to take a distributed perspective in practice. In doing so, the authors show us how, in the words of Kurt Lewin, "there is nothing as practical as a good theory," by demonstrating how theory can be very practical indeed in the hands of talented practitioners.

At the same time, this book is more than a guide to implementing distributed leadership, or an account about operationalizing distributed leadership in practice. The authors sell their work short in this respect. In several important ways, the authors flesh out important pieces of the distributed leadership puzzle, building out and filling in what it means to take a distributed perspective. Drawing on theoretical and empirical work on relational trust and work in teams, for example, the authors make important contributions to theoretical work on distributed leadership.

Most importantly, this book is based on a carefully-designed program of research, including a mixed-method cluster randomized control trial, and a replication study. It is unfortunate that this is the exception rather than the norm in books for policymakers and practitioners. The carefulness of the research design and execution makes the work all the more compelling. This book also reports on important empirical findings, such as the importance of combining professional development for leadership teams with organizational infrastructure design and redesign. Books that combine theory, research, and practice successfully are rare. This is one of those rare books, and as such it is essential reading for anyone interested in distributed leadership.

For practitioners and policymakers serious about distributed leadership this book is necessary reading. The authors offer tangible, research-based, guidance for practitioners and policymakers wishing to take a distributed perspective of school leadership and management. Moreover, the account is based on the authors' actual work of designing and implementing such a program in schools and school systems. It is based on their efforts to walk the talk of distributed leadership.

James P. Spillane
Chicago, September 2015

Preface

Until recently, the image we held of teaching was nearly ubiquitous. The teacher stands at the front of the room, chalk or pointer in hand. Students' desks are arranged in neat rows, facing forward. The blackboard or textbook is the primary tool for delivering information. Students are sitting and, if all goes well, listening quietly, occasionally advancing one at a time to work at the big board up front.

This reality has not disappeared either from our collective image of education or from the classrooms of today. But both how we think about teaching and learning, and what we see unfolding in the practice of teaching, have shifted dramatically. A now decades-old change is underway in how we understand the practice of instruction. Words and phrases such as *differentiation, small group instruction, student-centered pedagogy*, and *formative assessment* have become commonplace among teachers. Students are routinely graded on rubrics, often made available before an assignment is handed in. And in many classes you will see students engaging in Socratic seminars, working in small groups or independently at centers.

This shift is neither wholly new nor is it an even process, but it reflects at its core a deep change in how we understand instruction, and our grappling with the nature of teaching and learning. This has occurred under incredible pressure to reform schools; as international competitiveness has mounted, education has been positioned as a linchpin for politics and our economy, and we have worked to understand the continuously widening inequity in our public education system. All this has sharpened our focus on what we now see as the most important factor in predicting students' educational attainment: the quality of the teacher in the classroom.

Teacher Leadership, Shared Leadership: Shifts in Our Thinking about School Leadership

While teaching quality is a critical predictor of student achievement, teaching does not occur in a vacuum. The work of teaching must be organized. The teaching staff must be recruited and hired. Teachers who continually improve their craft collaborate with and receive feedback from each other, and from formal supervisors or coaches. Schools require resources and schedules. Organizational policies and procedures must be coordinated. Thus, in order to improve school achievement, our attention has turned to leadership.

For years, the school leadership field was dominated by a managerial perspective. Principals were the primary source of leadership and their duties were largely administrative. Then, instructional leadership rose in prominence. There was a growing recognition that the instructional and administrative functions of the school had to be linked. Effective schools could not treat these as parallel processes. Rather, decisions about staffing, budgeting, and resources had to inform and be informed by the instructional focus and needs of the school. An effective school leader, therefore, was an instructional leader who led a continuing conversation about teaching and learning.

But while principals must be instructional leaders, they cannot possibly be the only such leaders in their schools. This would require the principal to be both an expert manager and an expert pedagogue for each age group and subject area. This is impractical. Otherwise, for example, principals across common high-school campuses would need to understand and be able to lead physics class one moment, an advanced English class the next, followed by drama and musical education courses. The expectation that principals be content experts across all disciplines, not to mention the accompanying pedagogical approaches particular to each subject and field of study, is unreasonable. In reality, principals must know instruction, but they also must be able to tap into the knowledge and expertise of other educators.

Instructional leadership remains a cornerstone of our thinking about effective school leadership, but new pressures and opportunities have continued to broaden our perspective. The day-to-day expectations for school leadership are immense. In many schools this has come with the growth of site-based management, as individual schools display more control and autonomy in budgetary, curricular, and staffing decisions. Additionally, the continued rise of high-stakes testing alongside other policy changes has created new pressures around compliance and accountability, adding to the demands and pressure on school leaders.

The growing recognition that one leader cannot do it all has led to new frameworks for understanding school leadership, including those that emphasize teacher leadership approaches and strategies in schools. Models suggesting shared or reciprocal forms of leadership are increasingly popular. Among these, distributed leadership has received particular notice. But having a model is not enough. The true demand is for operationalized approaches to developing leadership capacity in schools—the kind of capacity that leads to school turnaround and systemic growth.

The Distributed Leadership Program

How to optimally develop leadership capacity in schools is one of the most pressing, relevant questions in education. Complementing the observation that leadership is critically important, an awareness of a crisis in the paucity of leadership talent (Davis, Darling-Hammond, LaPointe, & Meyerson, 2005), critiques of the inadequacy of our current systems for preparing and credentialing school leaders (Murphy, Young, Crow, & Ogawa, 2009), and dismal evaluations of our theoretical and empirical knowledgebase regarding the nature of and best practices for leadership development (Murphy & Vriesenga, 2004) are all currently manifest.

New leadership development programs continue to emerge in response to the state of the field (Bush, 2009). The Distributed Leadership (DL) Program of the Penn Center for Educational Leadership (PCEL), at the University of Pennsylvania, is one such example, leveraging the distributed perspective, combined with state-of-the-art research from across the spectrum of educational leadership, to build school leadership capacity (DeFlaminis, 2009). The distributed perspective is a framework for understanding leadership, which emphasizes the embedded, shared, and practice-oriented nature of organizational leadership. The program combines this perspective with a cohort model and the formation of school-based leadership teams, comprising school administrators and nominated teacher leaders. DL teams participate together in intensive in-service leadership training and professional development, and their work is supported at the school site by ongoing leadership coaching and focused strategic planning around instructional improvement goals identified collaboratively by school staff. At the school level, a more limited but targeted set of professional development sessions is also provided to the entire school staff, based upon identified areas of need. Leadership team in-service training is focused in the first year of the program implementation, but coaching, action planning, and faculty professional development continues through a three- to four-year implementation cycle.

Program Evaluation by the Consortium for Policy Research in Education

Through a partnership with the Consortium for Policy Research in Education (CPRE), an outside team of evaluators conducted a multiyear, randomized control trial (RCT) of the DL Program's effectiveness at driving school change. This work included quantitative data in the form of school and student metrics, and survey data from school staff. Qualitative data were drawn from interviews with participants and other staff members, observations and videotapes of team meetings, and written notes from coaching logs, feedback forms, and open-ended survey questions.

In addition to the formal evaluation conducted by CPRE, the DL Program was supported by the research of two then-doctoral students and co-authors of this volume, Mustafa Abdul-Jabbar and Eric Yoak. This comprised several pilot studies and research for the authors' doctoral dissertations.

These sources of research were augmented further by ongoing monitoring activities conducted by the program staff. The program's founder and Executive Director, John DeFlaminis, with Assistant Project Director, Jim O'Toole, and Project Coordinator, Lindsay Shafer, all collected ongoing feedback from program participants and leadership coaches. These data together were used to inform the successive iterations of the work described in Chapters 2 and 3.

In addition to providing information that was used to continually improve the implementation of DL projects, the implementation data also provide a source of more generalizable learning about key aspects of leadership.

About this Book

Implementation of the DL Program represents some of the most significant operationalizations of DL theory to date. In addition to building leadership capacity in DL schools, as confirmed through ongoing program evaluations, the DL Program offers a useful site to study the implementation of the distributed perspective in schools. Here, we wish to share with readers what we have learned in the nearly ten years since the program's inception. This book is designed either to be read in its entirety or to be accessed chapter by chapter, as best fits the reader's needs. While chapters do refer to and build upon each other, each also addresses a distinct aspect of either DL theory or the DL Program, all of which may be relevant to current and aspiring school leaders.

Part 1: A Distributed Approach to Leadership and Leader Development

The first three chapters are intended to introduce DL theory, as well as to demonstrate its operationalization through the DL Program.

Chapter 1: Distributed Leadership as a Framework for Learning and Practice

Chapter 1 introduces the concept of the distributed perspective: the theoretical foundation for the DL Program. DL theory is offered as a lens through which to view leadership, and a tool that developing leaders may use to reflect upon their own practice. We discuss what this looks like in schools, and enable the reader to better understand the conceptualization of the DL Program.

Chapter 2: Operationalizing Distributed Leadership: The Design, Implementation, and Replication of the Program

Chapter 2 discusses the design, implementation, and replication of the Distributed Leadership Program. This chapter documents the operationalization of distributed leadership in schools (*i.e.*, the move from distributed leadership theory to the practice of the same), focusing on how distributed leadership can be established in schools to support leadership development and school improvement. The chapter addresses the key structural and institutional levers utilized in the Distributed Leadership Program, and also presents findings from an independent evaluation of the DL Program and lessons learned from the field, identifying specific program components and leadership strategies that informed the DL Program's success.

Chapter 3: Leadership Theory into Practice: The Curriculum, Instruction, and Coaching in the Distributed Leadership Program

This chapter explores the instructional design of the DL Program. It offers a discussion of the content and focus of professional development sessions, and the integral role of coaches on DL teams. The chapter describes the seventy-seven hours of training deemed critical to the success of teacher leaders and principals, and explains how curriculum, instruction, and coaching supports can work together to promote effective teams and develop new school leaders.

Part II: Distributed Leadership for Building School Leadership Capacity

Part II describes what we have learned about leadership development more generally from the implementations and evaluations of the DL Program. Building upon the program findings, these chapters delve more deeply into what program participants experienced as they took on new leadership roles and collaborated on school-based leadership teams. This learning has important implications for the work of leader development in schools and in university-based preparation and certification programs.

Chapter 4: Distributed Leadership Teams: A Model for Team Leadership Development and Building Leadership Capacity in Schools

Chapter 4 discusses the role that DL teams, consisting of school administrators, teachers, and coaches, can play in developing leadership capacity and collegial community in schools. The chapter also distinguishes between professional learning communities in schools (PLCs) and DL teams, insomuch as both emphasize collaborative teaming strategies for school improvement.

Chapter 5: Scaling Leadership in Schools: The Development of Teacher Leadership Practice in Distributed Leadership Schools

Chapter 5 addresses the scaling up of leadership in schools through a strategic emphasis on teacher leader development. The chapter's thesis acknowledges that the traditionally flat leadership hierarchy of schools, led by one or two formal administrators and characterized by undifferentiated, largely isolated roles for teachers, is being destabilized by new pressures and opportunities to make school leadership practice more effective. The chapter offers lessons for the development of teacher leaders in the context of their site-based practice, and highlights how teacher learning can stimulate transformational change in schools.

Chapter 6: Learning to Trust, Learning to Lead: Implications for Leadership Development and Building Relational Trust in Schools

Chapter 6 explores lessons learned from the DL Program with regard to trust development in schools, practitioner-led change, relationship building, and shifting school climate. A feature of the chapter is that it provides a typology of specific leadership behaviors that promote trust in schools. School practitioners can use the typology framework to guide improvement planning that takes account of how trust can be nurtured to support change processes, and/or reform agendas in schools.

Part III: Distributed Leadership and Instructional Improvement

This final part looks to extend our thinking beyond the implementation of the DL Program, both to lessons for the field—including other schools interested in implementing a DL approach to leadership—and future directions for practice and research.

Chapter 7: Building Team and School Leadership Capacity: The Strategies and Routines that Work

The processes used to build team and school leadership capacity were different in every school, but drew upon a cluster of strategies that worked. This chapter addresses the common tools used by teacher leaders and administrators in the work of school improvement. While tailored to the needs of each school context, the DL Program provided common support structures and strategies to build team and school leadership capacity. This chapter describes these in detail, offering examples for schools and leaders seeking support in their DL-building process.

Chapter 8: Tips and Tools for Building School Leadership Capacity for Instructional Improvement

Chapter 8 provides tips, tools, and strategies for forming DL teams, creating action plans aligned with a school's instructional priorities, and determining the stages of DL development. While distributed leadership holds great potential for building school leadership capacity, to achieve instructional innovation and improve student learning, not all functions or decisions should be distributed. Thus, this chapter investigates distinctions between delegation and distribution, and between sharing tasks and sharing leadership. Furthermore, we discuss decision-making frameworks that leaders can employ to understand when, how, and why to involve others in decisions, and to distribute leadership in their schools.

Chapter 9: Revisiting the Distributed Leadership Program: Reflecting on Why/How it Worked as a Model for Leadership Development

This chapter highlights how the approach outlined in this book and operationalized in the DL Program can enable school leadership practice to make the twenty-first-century transition—moving away from rigid leadership roles toward networked coalitions of diverse actors in schools (including diverse professional teams of formal administrators, instructional coaches, teachers, and behavior support personnel). Chapter 9 topics include, but are not limited to, the following: moving beyond the "black box" of educational leadership practice, DL as a disruptive innovation, and networked/distributed systems of leadership. The primary intent in this chapter is to broaden the discussion on what constitutes efficient, effective organizational leadership, and why.

Conclusion

In this section, we offer a brief conclusory note, addressing the implications and takeaways of the DL Program. The authors encourage educational leadership practitioners to use this book as a practical tool for guiding reflection, promoting distributed leadership in their schools, and in their strategic planning for instructional improvement. To that end, the book offers chapter discussion questions, suggested readings, vignettes, and evidence from the field, and repeats instructive figures throughout the book along with other features intended for learners and practitioners of educational leadership who seek to build DL in their schools.

References

Bush, T. (2009). Leadership development and school improvement: contemporary issues in leadership development. *Educational Review, 61*(4), 375–389. http://doi.org/10.1080/00131910903403956.

Davis, S., Darling-Hammond, L., LaPointe, M., & Meyerson, D. (2005). *School leadership study: Developing successful principals* (Review of Research). Educational Leadership. Stanford, CA.

DeFlaminis, J. A. (2009). The design and structure of the building distributed leadership in the Philadelphia School District Project. Paper presented at the annual meeting of the American Educational Research Association. San Diego, CA.

Murphy, J., & Vriesenga, M. (2004). *Research on preparation programs in educational administration: An analysis.* Columbia, MO: University Council for Educational Administration.

Murphy, J., Young, M. D., Crow, G. M., & Ogawa, R. T. (2009). Exploring the broad terrain of leadership preparation in education. In M. D. Young, G. M. Crow, J. Murphy, & R. T. Ogawa (Eds.), *Handbook of research on the education of school leaders*. New York, NY: Routledge.

Acknowledgments

Our spouses, Patti, Maryam, and Laraine: our thought partners for their enduring patience and loving support.

Our colleagues, James O'Toole, Lindsay Shafer, and Jon Supovitz for their partnership and contributions throughout this work.

Our mentor and friend James Spillane, whose research, thinking, and teaching shaped this implementation.

The teacher leaders, administrators, and coaches of the Philadelphia and Archdiocese Schools, who believed in this program, trusted us, and made implementation happen.

The Annenberg Foundation, and Gail Levin, who funded the first project and guided the high standards for success.

Our parents, Elsie and Alfred DeFlaminis, Jamil and Fareedah Abdul-Jabbar, Margret O'Neall, and Stuart Yoak, whose sacrifices and belief in us gave us the motivation and education to achieve.

Our children, Alfred, John, Walí, Malik, and the children of Philadelphia, who were always on our minds and in our hearts as we worked to create more leadership capacity for a better education and future.

A Distributed Approach to Leadership and Leader Development

The chapters in Part I explain what distributed leadership (DL) is and how it can be used in school-based leadership practice. They include an in-depth review of the DL Program: an extensive program framework and implementation approach to operationalizing DL in schools. The DL Program approach offers practitioners a robust example from the field featuring a curriculum design framework which may provide further guidance for developing or complementing leadership preparation programs, particularly those that seek to include DL elements. DL theory and practice will be shown to provide a productive tool for individual leader development and reflection, as well as a novel, innovative way to reframe leadership practice.

Distributed Leadership as a Framework for Learning and Practice

Outstanding leadership has invariably emerged as a key characteristic of outstanding schools. There can no longer be doubt that those seeking quality in education must ensure its presence and that the development of potential leaders must be given high priority.

Beare, Caldwell, & Millikan, 1989, p. 99

In this chapter . . .

Introduction

Teaching is widely acknowledged to be the single most important factor related to student learning, but it does not occur in a vacuum. It is structured and supported by a host of organizational factors, effective leadership being foremost among them. Since the turn of the twenty-first century, mounting evidence has confirmed the direct and indirect effect of leadership on school effectiveness and student learning (Leithwood, Louis, Anderson, & Wahlstrom, 2004). These findings have led to increased pressure to ensure high quality leadership in schools (Darling-Hammond, LaPointe, Meyerson, Orr, & Cohen, 2007). However, despite knowing that leadership quality is important, understanding how it operates, and how it can be designed for in practice, can prove difficult.

According to Spillane, Halverson, and Diamond (2004, p. 4):

> While it is generally acknowledged that where there are good schools there are good leaders, it has been notoriously difficult to construct an account of school leadership, grounded in everyday practice, that goes beyond some generic heuristics for suggested practices. We know relatively little about the how of school leadership, that is knowledge of the ways in which school leaders develop and sustain those conditions and processes believed necessary for innovation.

While there is some broad agreement about what leadership is within organizations, why we need it, and which practices are most successful, there is much less consensus as to how it actually works. Bennis and Nanus (1997) argue that there are over 850 definitions of leadership, and that "no clear and unequivocal understanding exists as to what distinguishes leaders from nonleaders" (p. 4).

In light of these challenges facing the practice and understanding of educational leadership, this chapter opens Part I of the book with discussion on how leadership in schools has been perceived. It proceeds on this point by distinguishing between the prevailing, traditional view on leadership—the widely held view that leadership work in schools is performed primarily (if not only) by school administrators (*i.e.*, the "heroic leader" bias)—and a powerful emerging paradigm that has been termed the "distributed perspective" on leadership practice, or *distributed leadership* (DL). The chapter concludes with a discussion on how DL can serve as a tool for organizational design and leader development.

The "Heroic Leader" Bias

Leadership is still largely understood through a narrow lens. Most studies of school leadership continue to focus most often on formally appointed school leaders, principals, or assistant principals, and their actions and behavior. Numerous studies detail how school principals allocate resources, make decisions, incentivize and supervise other staff, and attempt to develop lists of the most important leadership actions (e.g., Waters, Marzano, & McNulty, 2003).

When we talk with teachers and administrators in schools, we find that hierarchical, top-down visions of leadership are prevalent. And though, increasingly, there are principals who work actively to foster staff collaboration, and teachers who perceive themselves to be leaders in their schools, nearly all still hold assumptions about leadership which emphasize formal leadership roles and top-down decision-making, with an emphasis on the actions of school principals. As a first-year principal describes, "You follow the pattern that you kind of lived under, which was the top-down—you make the decisions and you pass the decisions down" (Susie, personal interview, February 20, 2013). The pervasiveness of the top-down model of leadership across schools led one experienced teacher leader to comment that, "Leadership in any school I've been in has always relied on whoever the principal is" (Emily, personal interview, February 18, 2013).

These representations from the field are congruent with what Yukl (2010) has termed the "heroic leader" bias. The heroic leader bias refers to a view of leadership that associates leadership activity with *individual* practices and decision-making, without looking to broader and *collective* patterns of social interaction or contextual influences for examples of leadership practice. In this view, leadership is often equated with the actions and decisions of a few, formally appointed individuals, such that other sources of influence are ignored. They are simply not counted.

Table 1.1 The Traditional View of Leadership

Influenced by the "heroic leader" bias
● Leadership can be understood primarily through individual decision-making and actions.
● Leaders lead from the top by setting an example, or directing the actions of others.
● Leaders need to be strong, independent, and authoritative, and have expert knowledge of their field.
● Leadership is mostly aligned with the formal positions people hold within organizations like schools.
● Leadership is often associated with gendered and racialized perceptions of who holds social power and influence.

The heroic leader bias is widespread, deeply entrenched, and has influenced years of professional practice. This bias is shaped further by cultural context and stereotyped notions of ability along lines of gender, race, class, and national origin, similar to the *great man theories* of history. In the nineteenth century, Thomas Carlyle (1841) popularized the notion that major shifts across human history could be largely understood through the specific decisions and actions of a small number of particularly talented or influential men. While this view has since been widely criticized, it nonetheless reflects a longstanding bias in our world view and a widely held perception. As such, we find that "current leadership theories are biased in reflecting the structures and cultures of North American organizations run by White, Anglo, heterosexual men" (Chin, 2013). These biases tend towards underinclusiveness, narrowing our view not only of who leads, but also of what actions characterize leadership.

In short, that which is not counted, does not count. Thus, it is not surprising that the traditional view (summarized in Table 1.1) has resulted in numerous blind or blank spots in our understanding of how leadership works in schools (Hallinger & Heck, 1996; Spillane et al., 2004).

A New Vision for Leadership

While every leadership theory helps frame our perceptions and actions, there are dangers that attend the traditional, biased conception of leadership in the field. The misconception that leadership is primarily the province of formally appointed individuals causes others to overlook their own capacity for leadership. As such, they may fail to tap into their individual or collective power to drive change. Furthermore, this individualistic view is often context-insensitive; we may underappreciate the role of context and history in framing our actions. The notion that leaders are mainly authoritative decision-makers leads us to overidentify the individually talented and ambitious. And we may ignore other sources of power and undervalue those who foster relationships, build consensus, and lead from the middle as opposed to the front. These and other biases limit how we understand leadership and the actions we take to recruit and develop individual leaders, as well as foster collective leadership capacity within our schools.

Distributed leadership (DL) represents a move away from the heroic leader perspective and presents a new framework—the distributed perspective—that expands the definition and practice of leadership in organizations. The distributed perspective, discussed at length below, is more inclusive in its definition of leadership than the traditional, individualized view, and promises to broaden the practice of leadership, particularly because it overcomes the traditional view's problem of underinclusivity.

The Distributed Perspective

Our work with the Distributed Leadership Project has been informed most directly by the work and partnership of James Spillane and his collaborators (e.g. Spillane, 2006; Spillane & Coldren, 2011; Spillane et al., 2004). So, while we have also either worked with or drawn upon other theorists and commentators in the field, notably Alma Harris, Kenneth Leithwood, and Peter Gronn, it is upon Spillane's articulation of DL theory that we draw most directly. His definition of distributed leadership has been our working definition:

> Leadership refers to those activities that are either understood by, or designed by, organizational members to influence the motivation, knowledge, affect, and practice of organizational members in the service of the organization's core work.
>
> (Spillane, 2006, pp. 11–12)

What is significant in this definition is its scope: the fact that any and all activities *interpreted* or *intended* to influence organizational members in teaching and learning (*i.e.*, the core work of schools) are cognizable as *leadership activity*. More simply, this definition of leadership rather than pointing to any concrete, specific persons or individual actions (in contrast to the traditional view), casts a wider conceptual net, promoting a unique perspective on leadership that views all leadership activity as inherently "distributed," or "stretched over" the interactions of leaders and followers as they unfold within a specific social context (Spillane et al., 2004) (see Figure 1.1).

To say that leadership is *stretched* across (1) leaders, (2) followers, and (3) context is to suggest two things: interdependence and interaction. The notion of leadership being *stretched* focuses not just on the interdependence between these three components, but also on their interactions. Leaders, followers, and the situation are not static arrangements, but rather elements of a practice or performance unfolding dynamically in complex patterns over time. Just as expectations frame how a leader is perceived, so too do the actions of that leader frame current and future expectations. As the ways in which influence unfolds in organizations are often more fluid

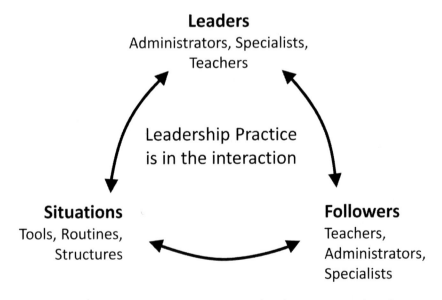

Figure 1.1 Leadership Practice as Constituted in the Interaction of Leaders, Followers, and Their Situation

Source: Adapted from Spillane, Halverson, & Diamond (2004, p. 11).

Table 1.2 Descriptive Versus Prescriptive Orientations

Descriptive	Prescriptive
Leadership *is* distributed	Leadership *should be* distributed

than we typically account for, focusing on these patterns of interactions can help to prevent us from framing leadership as static (or as yoked to static role assignments), promoting a more active, dynamic view of leadership practice.

Thus, the distributed perspective is just that: a perspective, a view, and a way of seeing or framing what we see. It is also descriptive rather than prescriptive, in that the distributed perspective does not tell us how leadership *should be* distributed but asserts that it already *is* distributed (Table 1.2).

We understand that leadership is about social influence and must be used to help the school set a direction and develop the human, organizational, and instructional resources to move towards that shared vision. Accounts differ, however, as to how this is accomplished. The distributed perspective emphasizes the *practice* and/or activity of leadership, the actions of and interactions among students, teachers, administrators, and other school community members. Rather than assuming that leadership flows from the principal, this perspective studies what happens in practice, and asks *how* leadership is actually accomplished.

The section below presents a vignette followed by guided reflection which make use of the distributed perspective to elucidate how the distributed lens can help organize our thinking about and response to leadership challenges.

Distributed Leadership Vignette

Principal Jones, in his first few months at Wayside Middle School, notices patterns across classrooms he has observed. Students demonstrate inconsistent ability to write a three-paragraph essay, often not understanding paragraph structure. Some write only one or two sentences, while others lump all their writing into one multi-page paragraph. Furthermore, this reflects inconsistency in teachers'

(continued)

9

(continued)

expectations. The Science Department has one rubric for grading essays, English teachers use another, and individual teachers offer different, even contradictory feedback to students.

As a past high-school English teacher himself, Mr. Jones feels well equipped to help his staff improve upon their instruction. At the next faculty meeting, he plans to introduce a new set of common expectations for teaching and grading essays across subject areas. Having revisited current research and best practices at other schools and considered alignment across grades, he feels well prepared.

Things start well that Tuesday afternoon. Reviewing progress that incoming students have made in the first months of school, teachers seem enthusiastic. But as the principal transitions into his presentation, he feels the energy start to shift. Some teachers are distracted or fidgeting. A few glance at others across the tables. Mr. Jones isn't sure why, but he notices that one English teacher, Ms. Mitchell, seems particularly tuned-out.

Teachers break into small groups, but the discussions seem shallow and fragmented. Mr. Jones observes several having side conversations or checking email. When everyone reconvenes to debrief, no one offers any direct opposition, but Mr. Jones senses that he won't see much of his plan implemented in classrooms that week. He is disappointed, unsure exactly what went wrong.

Heading back into his office, Mr. Jones is muttering under his breath. "What's wrong now?" quips the school secretary. "Oh, nothing. I'd just hoped that would go better," the principal starts, explaining his disappointment with the faculty meeting. "Well, that makes sense," the secretary replies, "but you should have seen it last year, when your predecessor and Ms. Mitchell had it out. She's really well-respected by the rest of the staff, a great English teacher. Without her on board, it's a tough sell to everyone else."

Consider the story of Principal Jones at Wayside Middle School and the three components of the distributed perspective. Who leads? In this example, the principal clearly believes he does. He has identified a problem, and he presumes to have the formal authority and institutional legitimacy to influence teachers. However, he encounters a different scenario in practice, unable to control influence upon the thoughts and actions of his teachers. Another school community member also carries influence, and teachers follow her reactions or behavior. Many communities are like this, with one or more Ms. Mitchells on staff holding formal roles or not, but wielding significant influence over others.

There are commonly multiple sources of influence within any one school community. From the distributed perspective, we observe that who actually leads may vary. Leaders may be individual, pairs or groups, formally appointed or not. They may lead for a long period or step up in response to a particular opportunity or need. At Wayside, Ms. Mitchell is an informal leader sharing influence with the principal, but they are not moving in unison. Each exerts influence, Ms. Mitchell perhaps unintentionally, yet neither leads as effectively individually as they might together.

So who follows? Some teachers may be "following" the example of Ms. Mitchell. If she is not on board with the new plan and engaged in the discussion, neither will they be. Others may be following the principal, but neither player generates great energy or movement. Ineffective leadership begets limited followership. While we often view "following" in a negative light, this example highlights the importance of having engaged followers in order for leadership to truly function.

And what is the situation? This often ignored element of school leadership is deeply complex but often tacit. The situation refers to the in-the-moment reality of the physical and social context, colored by the history of a place like a school and a community. Mr. Jones, unwittingly, knew little of the history of his school. Had he better understood its shared expectations, common beliefs, and existing relationships and power dynamics, he may have better led change. That his new idea was in the realm of writing instruction likely helped determine who else in the room would be an important influencer. Had the focus been on math or school culture, other community members may have emerged as formal or informal leaders. Similarly, we find that the day, time, and setting of events makes a difference. Are the staff energetic or tired? Are the expectations for a meeting widely shared, or is everyone on a different page? In short, situation plays an important role in the practice of leadership.

Table 1.3 Entailments of the Distributed Perspective

The distributed perspective, in summary:

- Leadership is not synonymous with formal roles or individual characteristics ("heroic perspective"). Leadership may vary per situation, often being shared across one or more formal and informal leader(s).
- Leadership does not reside solely in the decisions or actions of leaders. Rather, leadership practice is mutually constituted by the interactions between leaders and followers, and their situation.
- The distributed perspective does not say that leadership should be distributed, or that more widely distributed leadership is always better. Nor does it suggest that "everyone leads." Rather, it speaks to the ways in which leadership practice is distributed inherently, though the patterns of distribution may vary by situation.

As compared to other leadership theories, the distributed perspective stresses:

- Patterns of interactions as opposed to discrete actions.
- The role of followers in mutually constituting leadership practice.
- The role of the situation, including the designed or emergent tools, structures, and routines of an organization.
- The opportunity for multiple leaders to exist and work together in formal and informal roles.

Entailments of the Distributed Perspective

DL is both a theory of leadership practice and a theory born to tackle a particular set of problems in the field; namely, the "heroic" bias, and the need for a theory on how leadership actually occurs in schools. Table 1.3 summarizes key characteristics of the distributed perspective.

The Importance of Description

Again, the distributed perspective is primarily a descriptive framework. It underscores how reflection on organizational activity—what leaders and followers are doing at any given time, and how—can enhance our understanding and practice of leadership. When we act without reflecting on this bigger picture, we pass over opportunities to surface and question our current assumptions and beliefs about what, in fact, is occurring. This may inhibit our ability to more effectively understand and plan our response in any given situation. The hazard in this is that we may render our acts less effective.

For example, although one might initially assume that Wayside's Ms. Mitchell was a hindrance to leadership in her school because her attitude was not aligned with the formal leader's efforts, after reflecting on the situation using the distributed perspective, we realize that she is an untapped resource with powerful influence in her school. Focusing on description helps leaders and leadership observers better accommodate the way leadership unfolds in practice. Rather than moving from what we assume is happening, or from what we would like to happen, we are able to better understand what is actually occurring and to identify opportunities (e.g., untapped resources) in resolving leadership challenges.

Distributed Perspective on and in Practice

School leaders may take a distributed perspective both on and in practice. Spillane and Coldren (2011) refer to these as the reciprocal processes of "diagnosis and design." To say one takes a distributed perspective *on practice* is to suggest that one can come to view leadership through the DL lens, using DL to diagnose what one sees in their school. To take this perspective *in practice* is to use DL theory to drive leadership strategy and practices at the school or district level, using DL as a design framework for leadership. Using the distributed perspective both *on* and *in* practice can prove to be a powerful tool for practitioners, and can give rise to a self-refueling, recursive process of data-driven assessment and planning (Figure 1.2).

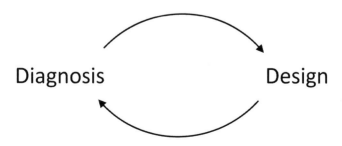

Diagnosis   Design

Figure 1.2 DL Cycles of Diagnosis and Design

As a tool for building school leadership capacity, the distributed perspective showcases both individual development and organizational design, to be explored across subsequent chapters. In the following sections we frame a few primary considerations and opportunities.

DL as a Tool for Leader Development

The distributed perspective helps us understand that individual, formal leaders are not the sole leaders in schools. This focus enables us to direct training and professional development resources to those in informal leadership roles, and to those who may be followers in any given situation. The distributed perspective helps us understand that formal leadership positions and actual leadership are "loosely coupled," particularly in education (Weick, 1976). They overlap but are not synonymous. Formal authority may be one of a school's many sources of leadership influence, but it is not the only source of such influence. In our leadership development work through the Distributed Leadership Program, we observed numerous opportunities for DL theory to benefit individual leader development for both school administrators and teacher leaders.

The Distributed Leadership Project purposefully operationalized what Spillane (2006) envisioned as the opportunity for DL in "principal preparation programs that work to develop a distributed mindset, helping principals to think about leadership practice and to think about it from a distributed perspective" (p. 98). We have seen how both principals and teacher leaders come to embrace aspects of the distributed perspective in their work, and the positive impacts this has on their leadership practices and their schools' capacity for instructional improvement (Abdul-Jabbar, 2013; Supovitz & Riggan, 2012; Yoak, 2013).

Reframing Leadership Roles and Expectations

The distributed perspective can help both principals and teacher leaders reframe leadership roles within their schools. Through participation in the DL Program, many teacher leaders and principal participants (though not all) came to reframe their notion of what it meant to be a school leader, and who they saw as leaders in their school. While most participants entered the DL Program with hierarchical notions of leadership, identifying leadership as primarily the work of formally appointed principals and assistant principals (the "heroic leader" paradigm), the new framework served as a doorway to a greater understanding.

For principals, this was often a process of acknowledging and fostering opportunities for co-leadership among teachers, administrators, and school community members. As one assistant principal describes:

> The thing I remember is really seeking to move towards allowing other people to drive the discussion, to do more of the facilitating piece—for a long time, our [principal] would set the agenda, guide the discussions, whereas for our three teacher leaders . . . I remember . . . waiting for them to guide the discussion. I remember having that clear thought about . . . breaking them of the habit of waiting for us [and] I think the other way is showing confidence in them, saying, 'I really feel like you can do this. Go do it,' and being there as a support. Whereas, I think in the past, it would have just been something that would have fallen to me.
>
> (James, personal interview, December 5, 2010)

As they came to take a more distributed perspective, administrators began looking for active opportunities to foster leadership in others, rather than simply waiting for it to happen or inviting collaboration.

For administrators, adopting the DL perspective in practice involved challenging old ideas and established models for leadership—both their own and those of their school community. They found that these changes often gained momentum as new ideas about leadership became more widely shared in their schools. One principal described this process:

> If you've empowered other people and you've set this up as this is our style of leadership here, then everyone assumes the responsibility, and everyone takes on that responsibility as their own and follows through on it, and it's shared responsibility. But it was hard to do that because it really was a change of my whole idea of leadership, as what I saw leadership as. [. . .] What I found invigorating about the DL Program for me and for our school situation was to change that whole approach where it doesn't always

start with me handing it down, but it starts with the distributed leadership group, and then it's a sharing of responsibility.

(Susie, personal interview, February 20, 2013)

While individual experiences shifted in different ways, these broad changes in how administrators came to understand leadership in their schools have been widely shared across many DL participants.

For teacher leaders, this process was largely about realizing their own leadership power. For many, this involved fighting against an established culture of individual isolation. As one teacher leader described:

Teachers are very within their own little world, and if you look beyond that, sometimes it's perceived that, "You need to kind of mind your own business and just worry about what you're doing within your own classroom" kind of mentality.

(Emily, personal interview, February 18, 2013)

Other teacher leaders talked about the organic or "natural" ways in which they had taken up leadership roles, primarily through sports, extra-curricular activities, or committee involvement. The biggest shift many realized was in considering themselves as leaders in their schools, and recognizing new opportunities to impact teaching and learning across classrooms directly and boost student achievement. As one teacher leader explained:

I think [the DL Program has] made me more willing to put forth effort and—not that I wouldn't want to put forth effort before— but to get involved in other things and to think outside the box for solutions to problems. I guess I see myself more as a leader in education, even if I go somewhere that isn't a DL school or isn't a school that has that method of or that model of working. I see myself more as an organizer and a coordinator of things than I do as just a classroom teacher in this room.

(Melisa, personal interview, February 4, 2013)

For teacher leaders, looking at school leadership through the distributed perspective allows them to re-evaluate their current roles, as well as their potential for exercising leadership influence beyond the walls of their classrooms.

Alongside a new appreciation for the leadership roles that teachers could play in schools, DL Program participants often represented shifts in understanding what it means to lead. These were mostly movements from seeing leadership as individual authority and expertise to understanding leadership as existing in multiple forms of influence. This experience also helped participants "surface and challenge" their existing mental models for leadership practice (Senge, 1990).

As one principal described:

> I think this work has pulled me even more, you know, beyond myself, but I think everybody brings – they have so many lenses. Like I have so many lenses I don't even know I'm wearing until something makes me aware of it.
>
> (Rita, personal interview, February 18, 2013)

This surfacing of the "lens" for leadership that participants held at the beginning of the program was an important precursor to redefining how they approached leadership in their schools. For example:

> I think when I became principal, I thought it was having to know best practices for instruction for teachers; being on the cutting edge of curriculum; being able to balance administrative duties; being able to inform teachers and provide in-services for them. So it was kind of like I had to be a Jack-of-all trades and a master-of-none type thing.
>
> (Rosalie, personal interview, July 27, 2011)

These "traditional" ideas of leaders as simply authoritative experts were challenged by the notions that, in a distributed perspective, there are multiple forms of influence, and the opportunity for both formal and informal leaders in different positions to play important roles. For teacher leaders, this often meant stretching their own perspective on their leadership practices. In particular, some became more confident in and adept at influencing others to drive school improvement:

> [Through the DL Program, I am] learning how to be very diplomatic about that and appealing, not in a manipulative way, to what everyone values.
>
> (S. Melisa, personal interview, February 4, 2013)

[It] really got me to think about being more open, and talking and collaborating with others. So in doing that, I was more confident to tell people in my group "Hey, why don't you do this, or hey, what will you think of that?" [The DL Program gave me] strategies for how to do it, strategies for being more confident, and being able to talk to other people.

(Sharon, personal interview, January 30, 2013)

DL as a Tool for Organizational Design

The distributed perspective also has particular implications for how we diagnose and design key aspects of the organizational structure of schools, and who is engaged in these processes. To this point, the DL Program largely operationalized the distributed perspective's diagnostic and design functions, by creating leadership teams whose primary work entailed practitioner reflection and action planning activities. These activities have reflected school leaders' success at better aligning leadership roles to impact the school community. One example includes tapping content-area experts within schools to lead staff professional development.

The distributed perspective revealed the existing structures and expectations in place at many schools. For example, many DL teams revisited how they used time during faculty meetings, shifting from an array of operational tasks to prioritizing time for instructional improvements.

Chapter Summary

Ultimately, the goal of DL theory is to offer a path forward to new and enhanced leadership practices, which help build the capacity of schools to improve instruction and raise student achievement.

The distributed perspective represents a powerful tool for looking at leadership practice. This perspective emphasizes the context-sensitive ways in which leadership as a practice is *stretched over* the interactions of leaders, followers, and their situation. This view informs diagnostic and design approaches to leadership development and practice, and can enable practitioners to recognize new opportunities to strengthen leadership practices.

In subsequent chapters, we will look more closely at how we can put this perspective to work in school leadership practice and leadership development. Specifically, we look to lessons learned in the design and replication of the DL Program, distilled across several iterations. We highlight principles from the field that are generalizable to a range of school contexts and leadership demands.

Chapter Discussion Questions

1. After reading Chapter 1, how do you now define a "school leader?" What opportunities for leadership are present in your school? How can you realize these opportunities?

2. Think of a leadership challenge you have experienced either in the past or currently. Using the distributed perspective, analyze the challenge. Are there any "untapped resources" or opportunities which present themselves? What are some strategies you can use to activate these opportunities?

Suggested Reading

- Gronn, P. (2003). *The new work of educational leaders: Changing leadership practice in an era of school reform*. Thousand Oaks, CA: Sage.

- Harris, A. (2007). Distributed leadership: Conceptual confusion and empirical reticence. *International Journal of Leadership in Education, 10*(3), 315–325. doi:10.1080/13603120701257313.

References

Abdul-Jabbar, M. (2013). *Distributed leadership and relational trust: Bridging two frameworks to identify effective leadership behaviors and practices* [Doctoral dissertation]. University of Pennsylvania. Available from ProQuest Dissertations and Theses database (UMI No. 35–62478).

Beare, H., Caldwell, B., & Millikan, R. H. (1989). *Creating an excellent school: Some new management techniques.* London; New York: Routledge.

Bennis, W. G., & Nanus, B. (1997). *Leaders: The strategies for taking charge.* New York, NY: Harper Business.

Carlyle, T. (1841). *On heroes, hero-worship, and the heroic in history.* London: Fraser, James.

Chin, J. L. (2013). Diversity leadership: Influence of ethnicity, gender, and minority status. *Open Journal of Leadership, 2*(1), 1–10.

Darling-Hammond, L., LaPointe, M., Meyerson, D., Orr, M. T., & Cohen, C. (2007). *Preparing school leaders for a changing world: Lessons from exemplary leadership development programs.* Stanford, CA. Retrieved from http://seli.stanford.edu

Hallinger, P., & Heck, R. H. (1996). Reassessing the principal's role in school effectiveness: a review of empirical research, 1980–1995. *Educational Administration Quarterly, 32*(1), 5–44. doi:10.1177/0013161X96032001002

Leithwood, K. A., Louis, K. S., Anderson, S. E., & Wahlstrom, K. (2004). *How leadership influences student learning.* New York, NY: The Wallace Foundation.

Senge, P. M. (1990). *The Fifth Discipline: The art and practice of the learning organization* (p. 412). New York, NY: Doubleday.

Spillane, J. P. (2006). *Distributed leadership.* San Fransisco, CA: Jossey-Bass.

Spillane, J. P., & Coldren, A. F. (2011). *Diagnosis and design for school improvement: Using a distributed perspective to lead and manage change* (p. 134). New York, NY: Teachers College Press.

Spillane, J. P., Halverson, R., & Diamond, J. B. (2004). Towards a theory of leadership practice: A distributed perspective. *Journal of Curriculum Studies, 36*(1), 3–34. doi:10.1080/0022027032000106726

Supovitz, J. A., & Riggan, M. (2012). *Building a foundation for school leadership: An evaluation of the Annenberg Distributed Leadership Project, 2006–2010.* Philadelphia, PA.

Waters, T., Marzano, R. J., & McNulty, B. (2003). *Balanced leadership: What 30 years of research tells us about the effect of leadership on student achievement.* Aurora, CO. Retrieved from http://www.educationalleaders.govt.nz/Pedagogy-and-assessment/Leading-learning-communities/

Balanced-Leadership-What-30-Years-of-Research-Tells-Us-About-the-Effect-of-Leadership-on-Student-Achievement

Weick, K. E. (1976). Educational organizations as loosely coupled systems. *Administrative Science Quarterly, 21*(1), 1–19.

Yoak, E. (2013). *Learning for leadership: Understanding adult learning to build school leadership capacity* [Doctoral dissertation]. University of Pennsylvania, Philadelphia. Available from ProQuest Dissertations and Theses database (UMI No. 36–10081).

Yukl, G. A. (2010). *Leadership in organizations* (7th edition). Upper Saddle River, NJ: Prentice Hall.

Operationalizing Distributed Leadership

The Design, Implementation, and Replication of the Program

In this chapter . . .

Overview of Operationalizing Distributed Leadership

Leadership matters. It is almost impossible to read *Education Week* or any education periodical without finding multiple references to leadership's importance for improving schools and promoting student learning. Leithwood, Seashore-Louis, Anderson, and Wahlstrom (2004), for example, found that "[l]eadership is second only to classroom instruction among all school-related factors that contribute to what students learn at school" (p. 5). And the Consortium on Chicago School Research at the University of Chicago identified leadership as the first essential support for school improvement (Sebring, Allensworth, Bryk, Easton, & Luppescu, 2006).

But, while leadership is important, a single administrator cannot adequately serve as an impactful instructional leader for an entire school without collegial support from teachers. Thus, engaging classroom teachers in the practice of leadership is particularly important in today's schools (Elmore, 2000; Lambert, Collay, Dietz, Dent, & Richert, 1997; Olsen, 2000; Spillane, Halverson, & Diamond, 2001).

To this observation, Leithwood and his colleagues (2006) found that school leadership has a greater influence on schools and students when it is distributed widely, and schools with the highest student achievement attribute their success, in part, to distributed sources of leadership (*i.e.*, school teams, parents, and students).

John DeFlaminis, Executive Director of the Penn Center for Educational Leadership (PCEL) and a co-author of this volume, drew upon his experience empowering and supporting school leaders during his superintendency of Pennsylvania's Radnor School District, while seeking to operationalize and develop a new school-leadership model focused on distributed leadership. The following section documents the development of the Distributed Leadership (DL) Program: a project implementation which translated educational leadership research and DL theory into practice.

Background for the Original Project

The original Distributed Leadership Project was funded originally in 2005, by a five-year grant from the Annenberg Foundation to the Penn Center for

Educational Leadership (PCEL). It was developed to operationalize a distributed perspective on leadership within a robust intervention in sixteen Philadelphia schools to create a stronger leadership fabric supporting school improvement (DeFlaminis, 2009, 2011, 2013). The Annenberg Distributed Leadership Project was one of the first efforts in the United States to deliberately take on the challenge of designing, operationalizing, and implementing a concerted effort to build distributed leadership capacity in a diverse set of urban schools, to improve the quality of teaching and learning. The successful program in Philadelphia schools led to a four-year replication in nineteen Archdiocese of Philadelphia schools, beginning in 2010, and a third replication and redesign in the York City School District in 2015.

The City of Philadelphia, which was identified by the United States Census Bureau as having the largest deep poverty population of the ten largest U.S. cities, was the site for the first project. When the project began in Philadelphia in 2004, Philadelphia was also among the largest school districts nationwide, with 190,000 students (K–12) enrolled in 263 schools. It had been identified then as one of the most socioeconomically, financially, and academically troubled school districts in the country. Unstable and inexperienced leadership also contributed to Philadelphia's woes, with nearly one out of five schools (forty-five across the Philadelphia public system) under the direction of a new principal. The project targeted newer school leaders and their teachers in our efforts to build distributed leadership teams, and build leadership capacity for Philadelphia schools.

The vision of the Annenberg Distributed Leadership Project was to redefine and reshape the role of school leadership in overburdened and complex urban schools. We believed that our focus on developing teacher leaders and building distributed leadership teams would complement and ensure the sustainability of other programs undertaken by the Philadelphia School District and other area universities. The project prepared principals and teacher leaders to function in distributed leadership teams, to improve instruction and achievement. That process was supported by extant leadership capacity, content coaching, school-wide development of professional learning communities, and routines focused on building and learning issues. In developing a model for distributed leadership training, and the support structures to sustain it, we believed that we would greatly increase the likelihood of the principals' and staffs' success in their schools. By working with teams in schools, we hoped to significantly impact system-wide efforts to improve instruction in each school.

Our Working Definition of Distributed Leadership

The work of James Spillane, a leading conceptualizer of leadership theory in the United States, influenced and guided the DL Program from inception. Spillane's definition of distributed leadership has been our working definition:

> Leadership refers to those activities that are either understood by, or designed by, organizational members to influence the motivation, knowledge, affect, and practice of other organizational members in the service of the organization's core work.
>
> (Spillane, 2006, pp. 11–12)

Since DL was relatively new in its implementation in schools, a specific research-based training and development plan did not exist that addressed our needs. Spillane's distributed perspective provided a framework for collaborative, task-oriented leadership practice that draws upon the expertise of multiple individuals. From a design perspective, the challenge was to develop structures and supports to enact that framework at the school level. Further, preparing teacher leaders and principals for building a distributed setting was an important priority. In the Distributed Leadership Program, this was achieved by creating distributed leadership teams in each site, and providing them with a carefully designed and extensive plan for training, leadership coaching, and effective routines that could enhance leadership capacity in each building.

Program Logic Model and the Theory of Change

The program logic model and theory of change guided our work in schools (this model had been developed before the grant began, and was further refined over time). Our logic model is shown in Figure 2.1. The first column depicts the contextual factors facing schools, which we know influence the experiences of both students and school faculties.

Philadelphia Distributed Leadership Initiative: Logic Model
Revised August 31, 2009

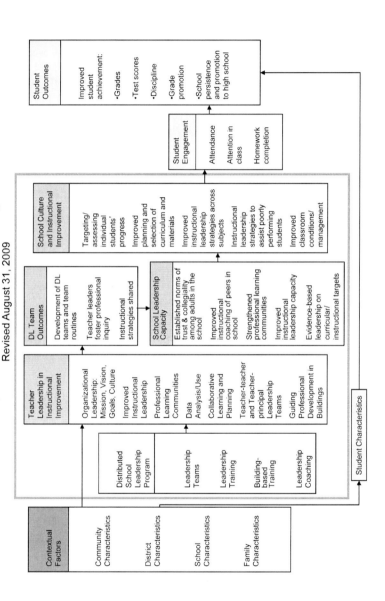

Figure 2.1 Distributed Leadership Program Logic Model

The second column shows program emphasis, where we build, train, and coach leadership teams to develop organizational leadership, instructional leadership, and professional learning communities, while also guiding professional development. We believed that these teams would foster professional inquiry and share instructional strategies, as well as build additional leadership capacity in the schools. These efforts did produce both culture change and instructional improvements in the schools, which contributed to both student engagement and student performance outcomes. The components inside the center box of Figure 2.1 are discussed later in this chapter, and in Chapter 3.

In addition to this program logic, we used a theory of change developed by our evaluators and the project director. This outlined a linear change process achieved in our original project, and represented expected outcomes for subsequent replications and our new teams.

Philadelphia Distributed Leadership Initiative: School-level theory of change

Revised August 31, 2009

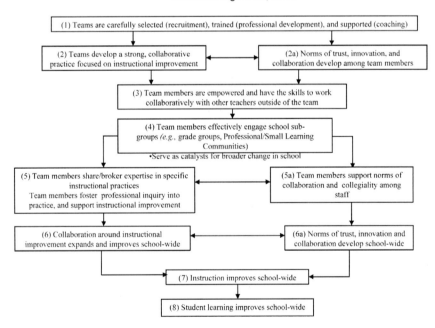

Figure 2.2 School-Level Theory of Change

Since these were targets of data collection and evaluation, they were excellent guides to implementation, and pleasing when found consistently in our projects. While the major outcome of improved student learning school-wide was not achieved in our first project, it was projected at a greater level in the second, as discussed in the *Lessons Learned* section of this chapter. More consistent outcomes of all projects to date are: teacher leadership in school improvement, team outcomes (in student achievement), school-leadership capacity growth, school culture change, and instructional improvement.

Distributed Leadership Project Design and Curricula

We spent the first year of our Annenberg grant conceptualizing plans for the work of the leadership teams, as well as the professional development experience that DeFlaminis intended for building their capacity to lead collaboratively. Since buildings would require a level of commitment that at times exceeded the contract, we believed that not only would agreements be needed with the district and the teachers union, but also with individual principals and teacher leaders. We required more than eight months to negotiate those agreements before we could start. All parties signed a memorandum of understanding which explores and clarifies all contract implications (for copies of the actual agreements, see DeFlaminis 2009 and 2011).

While this process created certain tensions and difficulties, it was an important element of our design, and the project enjoyed collaborative and positive support from the district and the Philadelphia Federation of Teachers. This work anticipated and resolved conflict and contract issues before they occurred. These understandings were used in all subsequent replications and we experienced no contract problems.

Program Overview

The Annenberg Distributed Leadership Project both conceptualized and developed the distributed leadership intervention. We trained almost

100 DL team members in 16 Philadelphia schools (10 elementary, 1 middle, and 5 high schools), across three cohorts in 2005, and later replicated the same project in 19 Archdiocese of Philadelphia schools (15 elementary and 4 high schools) in 2010. The project oversaw the development of a comprehensive, professionally produced curriculum (addressed extensively in Chapter 3), which provided extensive training (77 hours of leadership training, plus 40 hours of school-based instructional professional development), and leadership coaching to school-leadership teams. While support was most intensive in the first year, teams continued to participate in the program for the length of the two projects.

Why Teams?

From DeFlaminis' experience as superintendent of a high-achieving school district, we learned the power of teams. He used teams both to increase buy-in and improve quality of many decisions; to improve planning and coordination; and to improve classroom-level support for instructional change. Michael Fullan (2005), in his book about leadership and sustainability, discusses capacity building, and explains that providing workshops and professional development for all is not enough. Daily collaboration is still necessary. Teams cannot learn objectives from a workshop or course, but rather by doing them and designing mechanisms for improving them purposefully. Schmoker (2006) believes that talent and sustained commitment are most apt to be successful in team settings that combine autonomy and responsibility for better results, and enable individuals to share their collective and complementary skills and abilities. Richard Hackman's (2002 and 2009) work on teams also provided important guidance for the development of distributed leadership teams. Hackman identified five basic conditions that leaders must fulfill in order to create and maintain effective teams:

1. Teams must be real and people must know who is on the team;
2. Teams need a compelling direction;
3. Teams need enabling structures clear tasks and norms;
4. Teams need a supportive organization;
5. Teams need expert coaching.

Both the literature on leadership teams and DeFlaminis' positive experiences with them contributed to the construction of the DL development experience.

DL views building leadership capacity as a school-wide endeavor requiring high levels of interaction and collaboration among staff. To accomplish this, the Distributed Leadership Program first creates leadership teams that are collaborative, strategic, and instructionally focused to identify and prioritize school needs, define the leadership work necessary to address those needs, and establish feedback systems to monitor their progress. Individual team members create leadership opportunities and support teachers as they take on leadership tasks. Effective implementation requires that distributed leadership teams: (a) have a strong conceptual grounding in DL; (b) are highly collaborative; (c) know how to facilitate change in others; (d) are comfortable using data to both plan and monitor their work; and (e) focus on instruction.

School personnel must think about teams as one thinks about distributed leadership in a building. Elmore (2003) explains that powerful leadership is distributed because the work of instructional improvement is distributed. Schools that are improving seldom, if ever, engage exclusively in role-based professional development—that is, professional learning in which people in different roles are segregated from one another. Instead, learning takes place across roles. Improving schools pay attention to who knows what, and how that knowledge can strengthen the organization (Elmore, 2003). It is our belief that DL teams can accomplish that end in a more effective and coordinated way, to improve learning.

Distributed leadership is a form of collective leadership in which practitioners work collaboratively to develop expertise. This contrasts with traditional leadership notions in which an individual manages hierarchical systems and structures. This distributed view of leadership requires schools to "decentre" the leader (Gronn, 2003), and to subscribe to the view that leadership resides not solely in that individual at the top, but in every person at entry level who in any way acts as a leader (Goleman, Boyatzis, & McKee, 2002). A contrast of the traditional model and the distributed model intended in this development can be found in Appendix C, "Moving to a Distributed Leadership Structure: A Checklist." This development process is helpful in explaining to new teams how the evolution of the DL team occurs.

We designed each training module to prepare the leadership teams to relate to and support distributed leadership theory and effective teacher leader practice. The initial goals were to cultivate teams which function autonomously as professional communities, and to develop routines focused on instructional leadership and improvement. These teams served as a catalyst for broader change in the school, both by sharing their expertise in specific instructional practices and by working to establish and support norms of collaboration and collegiality among school staff. These practices foster professional inquiry into practice and support instructional improvement. Through 40 hours of professional development, targeting need-specific building and staff instructional needs, the teams promoted expanded instructional leadership by their colleagues.

Distributed Leadership teams were formed through an interview process requiring interested schools to first agree to the project and secure a two-thirds vote of the faculty. Interested individuals submitted applications, which were reviewed by the principal, the Project Director, and the Assistant Project Director. Interviews involving the same three reviewers used a protocol developed by the project team (see Appendix A). Appointment required the approval of the principal. The teams were typically comprised of three to seven individuals, including the principal and assistant principal(s), with all receiving stipends.

Evaluation and Replication of the Distributed Leadership Program

The continuation and replication of the Distributed Leadership Program has occurred based on positive evidence from the original Annenberg Project, confirmed by a rigorous mixed-method cluster randomized control trial (Supovitz & Riggan, 2012) conducted by the Consortium for Policy Research in Education (CPRE). For an electronic copy of this report, see http://www.cpre.org/building-foundation-school-leadership-evaluation-annenberg-distributed-leadership-project-2006-2010.

The strongest evidence of the program's impact on the distributed leadership teams and their work comes from survey data comparing leadership teams in the DL schools relative to those in comparison schools. These data show overwhelming and statistically significant differences between the DL teams and the leadership teams in the comparison schools, on a number of leadership team outcomes. These included: measures of effective team functioning; school leaders' sense of efficacy; trust levels among team members; trust levels between team members and their principal; perceptions of school influence; teacher satisfaction; and member learning opportunities (Supovitz, 2009). These findings, supported by data from a variety of sources, focused on high-functioning leadership teams and provide evidence that DL impacted both team effectiveness and culture (Supovitz & Riggan, 2012). The data showed that culture was impacted significantly in a two-year time frame. Specifically, the experimental evidence of improved team culture was statistically significant, supported by findings in the following areas: trust, collective responsibility, efficacy, influence, satisfaction, and opportunities to learn.

The Distributed Leadership Project also demonstrates that an intensive effort to influence and expand the leadership capacity of schools can have a positive impact on leadership practice, leadership team functioning, and support for instructional improvement. The positive impacts on the instructional practice of teachers, targeted by team members' action plans, provides evidence of leadership team functioning and support for instructional improvement (Supovitz & Riggan, 2012). One of our best examples came from a first project principal in a vocational high school, who explains how her team accomplished this:

> Teachers in academic classes that have completed the benchmarks in science, math, and English are analyzing the data to ensure that they are targeting the students' weakness. By targeting the students' weakness, teachers are able to re-adjust their instructional program and re-teach their prominent areas of weakness. Teachers also analyze their teaching methods by completing the benchmarks protocol analysis, thereby allowing them to improve their teaching skills, and to differentiate their instruction by using various teaching strategies. The aim of the teachers is to help every student to meet mastery and academic success in their content areas. There have been dramatic changes in the overall conversation among staff as it relates to planning and sharing with each other . . . The team has evolved and members are more willing to offer their input as roles change and individuals

work on a common mission. [The] DL team has established themselves as a viable entity within the school structure . . . The professional development sessions are moving along quite well. Our conversations are more focus [sic] and directed to outcomes to support student achievement . . . Teachers are more open to sharing and supporting their instructional practices and strategies with colleagues. The meetings are now a part of the culture of the school . . .

Finally, evidence from the last Archdiocese project has documented that the program stimulated changes in leaders' thinking about leadership (Yoak, 2013). The content and experience of the program challenged past ways of thinking and doing. The latter produced abundant evidence of projects often completed in schools faster than usual, as a result of trust built, and reculturing and restructuring in a DL context (Abdul-Jabbar, 2013). Abdul-Jabbar concluded (2013) that "trust was a critical component in advancing and speeding up a leadership team's progress" in a school improvement and school change effort.

Lessons Learned and Beliefs Confirmed

We have learned many lessons and confirmed many beliefs in our last eleven years doing this work, all discussed in a presented paper (DeFlaminis, 2013).

Lessons Learned

1. The principal's support was essential to, but not always sufficient for, the success of a distributed leadership school.

2. The Central Office's support was not essential to the continuing success of a school distributed leadership team.

3. Agreements with the unions about contract issues and role expectations for principals and teacher leaders greatly supported our success.

4. A distributed-leadership focus on instructional improvement required that the district had a coherent curricula, instructional plan, and authentic literacy and assessments in place, in order to achieve gains

in measured student outcomes. Progress in instructional practices and school improvements did occur without these requisites.

5. Action plans were useful routines to crystallize the teams' knowledge and intent, and to monitor progress.

6. Trust was a critical component in advancing and speeding up a leadership team's progress in a school-improvement project.

7. Distributed leadership teams were able to accelerate the focus and action on important instructional and school-wide priorities.

Beliefs Confirmed

1. Distributed leadership can be operationalized successfully in randomly selected, urban schools, including high schools.

2. The best professional development occurs within the context of schools and systems through team-led, building-based planning.

3. A teacher leader's motivation was an important element of their commitment and effectiveness in operationalizing distributed leadership.

4. Leadership coaching was an effective source of support for complex interventions and context issues.

5. Effective teacher leaders could be found in every school and many are already well-developed.

6. People support what they help to create.

7. Effective leadership occurs when the needs of the leader and those being led are satisfied.

Lessons Learned Point 4 (see above) has substantially impacted our work in all sites, but especially in York, Pennsylvania, the site of the latest replication of the DL Program, and is discussed below.

Highlights of a Critical Lesson

A distributed-leadership focus on instructional improvement required that the district had coherent curricula, instructional plan, and authentic literacy and assessments in place, in order to achieve gains in measured student outcomes. Progress in instructional practices and school improvements did occur without these requisites, but not to the extent intended.

Mike Schmoker (2011), in his book *Focus: Elevating the essentials to radically improve student learning*, maintains that three simple things are "essential" for schools: reasonably coherent curricula (what we teach); sound lessons (how we teach); and far more purposeful reading and writing in every discipline, or authentic literacy (integral to both what and how we teach). In addition, he recommends checks for understanding or formative assessments as critical to a lesson's success. Schmoker maintains, "as numerous studies demonstrate, these three essential elements are only rarely implemented; every credible study confirms that they are still pushed aside by various initiatives every year, in the majority of schools" (2006, p. 2).

When we began the Annenberg Project, we met with Central Office leaders to develop understanding and support, and to reduce conflict and redundancies. Central Office told us to develop strong teacher-leadership capacity and outcomes targeted at instructional improvement. We should not focus on curriculum or instructional strategies as the district "planned to have them in place," and would implement training. We used the same consultant for professional learning communities to avoid conflict in theory or practice. The curricula were revisited and strengthened in those early years, but no plans for instruction or formative assessments were ever put into place, through any of the three changes in superintendent (and other lay leaders') leadership. We added training late in the Annenberg Project with the Penn Literacy Network (year 4), because buildings requested instructional support. This never made up for the district's lack of a coherent plan for learning, including both curricula and instruction, and impacted our results and effects on student learning. While we saw impressive effects on individual projects and action plans, we never realized the extent of student effects anticipated.

The Archdiocese, further along in its infrastructure "essentials," was moving to the Common Core Standards, while developing curricula, and training the entire district on Understanding by Design. Once our leadership modules were completed, virtually all of the building-determined professional development requested was targeted to the Archdiocesan priorities and training. The teams were able to support their schools and colleagues in understanding and implementing these new initiatives, which would be measured with new standardized exams. Action plans focused most often on incremental success in moving forward, and hence supported both the essentials and targeted student outcomes.

Yoak and Abdul-Jabbar found evidence in Archdiocesan schools that distributed leadership work was impacting the teams' and the schools' instructional practices. They explain:

> In our work with our research participants, all respondents reported strong effects for the impact of a distributed approach to leadership on their own and their school's instructional practices . . . as their understanding of more effective instructional practice developed, their routine practices evolved which were then further related to improvements in, and changes to, organizational structures, instructional practices, student and staff learning, and observations of improved school culture.
>
> (Yoak & Abdul-Jabbar, 2011)

In our latest project in York, Pennsylvania, it is essential that teams bring leadership to the infrastructure of the educational system (curricula, instruction, formative assessments, and a strong literacy plan). We decided to begin by auditing these areas to gauge where the district stood. On this project, we are building parallel projects and capacities in distributed leadership and educational infrastructure. Spillane has defined infrastructure as "those structures and resources that are mobilized by school systems and school organizations to enable (and constrain) classroom teaching, maintain instructional quality, and lead instructional innovation" (Spillane, 2008, Module 2: Unit 4, Slide 6) and has pointed out that "design of the formal organization infrastructure shapes the informal organization." Our goal is to effect school improvement and to affect school culture to build a better system for student achievement. In this way, we can be assured that essentials will be in place as the leadership teams work with buildings to improve schools and student achievement within.

Chapter Summary

Distributed leadership can be successfully operationalized in K–12 urban schools. The results of a rigorous mixed-method cluster randomized control trial in the first project provided ample evidence that leadership teams could make a difference. The first project documented and the second project replicated that the efforts to influence and expand the leadership capacity of schools can positively impact leadership practice, leadership team functioning, and support for instructional improvement. Both projects showed that Distributed Leadership impacted culture significantly in a two-year time frame. Finally, we learned that leadership development must go hand in hand with infrastructure development to have optimal effects on student achievement.

Chapter Discussion Questions

1. Reflect on Hackman's five basic conditions with respect to teams you have been a part of, or led. To what extent do you believe these conditions were present? Do you believe the presence of these conditions enhanced (or would have enhanced) the effectiveness of your team? Why/why not?

2. Using the program logic model in Figure 2.1, explain how teacher leadership is used as a lever for building leadership capacity in schools.

Suggested Reading

- Briggs, K., Davis, J., & Cheney, G. R. (2012). The promise of a strong principal. *Education Week*, May 9.
- DeFlaminis, J. A. (2013). *The implementation and replication of the Distributed Leadership Program: More lessons learned and beliefs confirmed.* Paper presented at the annual meeting of the American Educational Research Association, San Francisco, CA.
- Newman, F., King, B., & Youngs, S. P. (2000). *Professional development that addresses school capacity: Lessons from urban elementary schools.* Paper presented to Annual Meeting of the American Educational Research Association, New Orleans, LA.
- Schmoker, M. (2011). *Focus: Elevating the essentials to radically improve student learning.* Alexandria, VA: Association for Supervision and Curriculum Development.

- Spillane, J. P. (2006). *Distributed leadership*. San Francisco, CA: Jossey-Bass.
- Spillane, J. P. (2008). *The distributed perspective: Modules one and two of the distributed leadership series*. Developed and Supported by a grant from the Carnegie Corporation.
- Spillane, J. P., & Diamond, J. B. (2007). *Distributed leadership in practice*. New York, NY: Teachers College Press, Columbia University.
- Supovitz, J., & Riggan, M. (2012). *Building a foundation for school leadership: An evaluation of the Annenberg Distributed Leadership Project, 2006–2010*. Consortium for Policy Research in Education, University of Pennsylvania.

References

Abdul-Jabbar, M. (2013). *Distributed leadership and relational trust: Bridging two frameworks to identify effective leadership behaviors and practices* [Doctoral dissertation]. University of Pennsylvania. Available from ProQuest Dissertations and Theses database (UMI No. 35–62478).

DeFlaminis, J. A. (2009). *The design and structure of the building distributed leadership in the Philadelphia School District Project*. Paper presented at the annual meeting of the American Educational Research Association, San Diego, CA.

DeFlaminis, J. A. (2011). *The design and implementation of the Annenberg Distributed Leadership Project*. Paper presented at the annual meeting of the American Educational Research Association, New Orleans, LA.

DeFlaminis, J. A. (2013). *The implementation and replication of the distributed leadership program: More lessons learned and beliefs confirmed*. Paper presented at the annual meeting of the American Educational Research Association, San Francisco, CA.

Elmore, R. (2000). *Building a new structure for school leadership*. Washington, DC: The Albert Shanker Institute.

Elmore, R. (2003). A plea for strong practice. *Educational Leadership, 61*(3), 6–10.

Fullan, M. (2005). *Leadership and sustainability: Systems thinkers in action.* Thousand Oaks, CA: Corwin Press.

Goleman, D., Boyatzis, R., & McKee, A. (2002). *The new leaders: Transforming the 'art of leadership into the science of results.* London: Time-Warner.

Gronn, P. (2003). *The new work of educational leaders: Changing leadership practice in an era of school reform.* London: Paul Chapman.

Hackman, J. R. (2002). *Leading teams: Setting the stage for great performances.* Boston, MA: Harvard Business School Press.

Hackman, J. R. (2009). In D. Coutu, Why teams don't work. *Harvard Business Review, 87*(5), 103.

Lambert, L., Collay, M., Dietz, M. E., Dent, K., & Richert, A. E. (1997). *Who will save our schools? Teachers as constructivist leaders.* Thousand Oaks, CA: Corwin Press.

Leithwood, K., Mascall, B., Strauss, T., Sacks, R., Memon, N., & Yashkina, A. (2006). Distributing leadership to make schools smarter. *Leadership and Policy, 6*(1), 37–67.

Leithwood, K., Seashore-Louis, K., Anderson, S., & Wahlstrom, K. (2004). *How leadership influences student learning: A review of research for the Learning from Leadership Project.* New York, NY: Wallace Foundation.

Lubrano, A. Of big cities, Philadelphia worst for people in deep poverty. *Philadelphia Inquirer,* March 20, 2013.

Olson, L. (2000). Principals try new styles as instructional leaders. *Education Week, 20*(9), 1 & 15.

Schmoker, M. (2006). *Results now: How we can achieve unprecedented improvement in teaching and learning.* Alexandria, VA: Association for Supervision and Curriculum Development.

Schmoker, M. (2011). *Focus: Elevating the essentials to radically improve student learning.* Alexandria, VA: Association for Supervision and Curriculum Development.

Sebring, P. B., Allensworth, E., Bryk, A. S., Easton, J. Q., & Luppescu, S. (2006). *The essential supports for school improvement.* Chicago: Consortium on Chicago School Research.

Spillane, J. P. (2006). *Distributed leadership.* San Francisco, CA: Jossey-Bass.

Spillane, J. P. (2008). The Distributed Perspective: Module two of the Distributed Leadership Series: From diagnosis to design, module 2. Evanston, IL: The School of Education and Social Policy, Northwestern University.

Spillane, J. P., Halverson, R., & Diamond, J. (2001). Investigating school leadership practice: A distributed perspective. *Educational Researcher, 30*(3), 23–29.

Supovitz, J. A. (2009). *Distributed leadership evaluation memo.* Consortium for Policy and Research in Education. Philadelphia, PA: University of Pennsylvania.

Supovitz, J., & Riggan, M. (2012). *Building a foundation for school leadership: An evaluation of the Annenberg Distributed Leadership Project, 2006–2010.* Consortium for Policy Research in Education, University of Pennsylvania.

Yoak, E. (2013). *Learning for leadership: Understanding adult learning to build school leadership capacity* [Doctoral dissertation]. University of Pennsylvania, Philadelphia. Available from ProQuest Dissertations and Theses database (UMI No. 36–10081).

Yoak, E., & Abdul-Jabbar, M. (2011). *A distributed approach to leadership development: How leaders construct conceptual frameworks for practice.* Paper presented at the University Council for Educational Administration Annual Conference, Pittsburgh, Pennsylvania.

Leadership Theory into Practice

The Curriculum, Instruction, and Coaching in the Distributed Leadership Program

In this chapter . . .

Overview of Leadership Theory into Practice

To prepare and support the distributed leadership (DL) teams and team members to carry out their work, the DL Program provided schools with intensive professional development, instructional materials, and ongoing coaching support. This chapter describes the 77 hours of training that was deemed critical to the success of teacher leaders and principals as they engaged in DL, in both the School District of Philadelphia and the Archdiocese of Philadelphia. The chapter provides an overview of the rationale for the modules developed for practitioner learners of DL (distilled from a seven-year study by Spillane, 2006, and Spillane et al., 2007 and 2008), and further provides a descriptive account of each module. The professional modules were instructionally designed for greater effectiveness and were delivered to teacher leaders, principals, and coaches, in order to create a common understanding that could influence their behavior and schools. The chapter explains how each module contributed to the overall training plan used in the DL Program that was intended to help teacher leaders and campus personnel be more skillful as individuals, and create teams where these skill sets complemented others.

In this chapter, we also explore how coaches' roles are instrumental to effective teams and new leader development. Leadership coaching is a critical strategy for creating and sustaining effective teams (Hackman, 2009). Distributed leadership coaches are experienced leaders who receive training with their teams and attend team meetings, while also working with individual team members as needed.

Finally, this chapter will describe how the DL Program supported teacher efficacy. The development of skilled individual leaders and strong leadership teams, using a robust leadership curriculum, combined with engaging instruction and ongoing coaching, bolstered the enactment of distributed leadership in schools. The approach depicted in this chapter is instructive for practitioners designing professional development opportunities that support a DL approach, and offers guidance for those seeking to implement DL in leader development programs or at the school site.

Leadership Training/Curricular Modules for Capacity Building

An increasing body of evidence points toward the importance of capacity building as a means of developing and sustaining school improvement (Fullan, 2001; Sergiovanni, 2001). A key step in operationalizing a DL plan requires building key skills in principals, teacher leaders, and coaches that would realize greater leadership capacity overall. In establishing the DL Program our guiding question was: "What would teacher leaders need to know and be able to do to be successful in a distributed leadership school?" Our response to this question led to the development of 70 hours of leadership training delivered throughout year one in modules and ranging from 3.5 hour sessions (half day), to 7 hours (full day), to 14 hours (two full days). Later in the project, peer coaching was added as a full-day experience, accounting for the total 77 hours of leadership training.

Training was front-loaded through a week-long summer session, which included two days of training on Distributed Leadership, and another two days focusing on professional learning communities, and team and trust development. A fifth day focused on data analysis and use. Full- and half-day training was then conducted throughout the school year, to focus on topics such as mission and direction, teamwork and conflict resolution, and leadership of literacy and mathematics. In addition to these modules, DL teams received continuous support from a leadership coach throughout the school year. Table 3.1 shows the topics of each training module and their length.

The topic of each training module was designed to prepare the leadership teams for issues related to and supporting DL theory. The initial

Table 3.1 Distributed Leadership Program Curriculum Modules

Ref	Title	Length (hours)
1	**Distributed Perspective** Learn about the Distributed Perspective of Leadership, which includes: leadership practice as the central and anchoring concern; leadership practice as generated in the interactions of leaders, followers, and their situations; and how the aspects of the situation both contribute to defining leadership practice and are defined through leadership practice.	14.0
2	**Developing Professional Learning Communities** Learn about effective learning communities, including how to link the work of professional learning communities with student achievement, building community and trust, protocols for looking at student work, the elements of a good rubric, and practice writing a rubric.	14.0

(continued)

Table 3.1 (continued)

Ref	Title	Length (hours)
3	*Mission and Direction: Shared Vision, Values, and Commitments* Learn how to delineate the role that leaders play in developing vision and goals, and sustaining them for their schools. Learn how to consider stakeholder roles from a cultural perspective, when defining mission and vision.	3.5
4	*Emotional Intelligence* Learn how to work well with others, have self-confidence, bounce back from difficulties, empathize with how others are feeling, and control your emotions.	3.5
5	*Building District Leadership Teams* Learn about team-building, which commits people to engage in patterns of behavior, and produces performance that results in desired outcomes.	3.5
6	*Teamwork and Conflict Resolution* Learn the types of conflict and approaches to managing conflict in an effort to obtain cooperation in attaining goals.	3.5
7	*Building Bridges and Connections* Gain a multifaceted understanding of concepts and practices for engaging different stakeholders in improving student learning. This module focuses on different engagement practices and how to apply them inside, as well as outside, your school.	3.5
8	*Evidence-based Leadership Using Data to Guide School Improvement* Learn how to use data effectively to inform decision-making, provide effective feedback, and review the use of data modeling tools. You will identify ways to make innovative use of student-performance data at your school.	7.0
9	*Leadership for Literacy Teaching and Learning* Learn how to define literacy within the context of your work, review best practices for school-wide literacy practices, explore research-based literacy strategies, and draft an action plan for literacy leadership.	3.5
10	*Motivation: The Key to Effective Leadership* Understand motivation and how it evolved as a process over time; develop an understanding of the elements of motivation and how each can be managed in a school setting, and the connections between the elements of motivation, motivating colleagues and functioning as a distributed leadership team.	3.5

11	**Fostering Leadership in Mathematics** Learn how to identify directions for mathematics learning to propose for your school, consider best practices in mathematics education, and understand changes in mathematics education.	3.5
12	**Collaborative Learning Cultures** Learn about collaboration, including the current status of collaboration in your school, possible resisters, structures and tools that can be used to sustain collaboration, and how to develop a theory of action that builds the collaborative capacity of your team and staff as a whole.	3.5
13	**Developing Evidence-based and Shared Decision-making** Learn about and understand the mental models that impact our thinking, and the role of data in decision-making; use data to improve the quality and acceptance of your team's decision; and explore models that can help the distributed leadership team to understand when and how to involve others in shared decision-making.	3.5
14	**Peer Coaching** Learn about peer coaching, which has been identified as one of the most effective practices to ensure transfer of training (to 80% learning). Learn effective strategies and techniques for working with colleagues in a peer-coaching context.	7.0
	Total Number of Module Hours	77.0

goal was to cultivate teams that functioned autonomously as professional learning communities, and to develop routines focused only on instructional leadership and improvement. These teams served as a catalyst for broader change in the school, by both sharing their expertise in specific instructional practices and by working to establish and support norms of collaboration and collegiality among school staff. This fostered professional inquiry and supported instructional improvement. One first project principal explained how DL team member activity engaged other staff in her building:

> The team members continue to improve their teaching practices by reading current research and implementing new strategies. Team members also share information and new instructional innovations with their colleagues. The DL team remains committed to improving the quality of teaching and learning through

designing and planning professional development, mentoring, and coaching.

Two teachers, who are not DLT members, took the initiative and led professional developments. This is further evidence of how the DL has influenced other teachers to do more than teacher [sic] in their classrooms. They feel empowered to share and conduct workshops around best practices. It is very rewarding to me to see how our Distributed Leadership Team members have developed their leadership skills as the year has progressed. I enjoy watching them assume leadership responsibilities, and listening to them discuss ways in which they can coach and support their colleagues, as well as share their knowledge with peers.

I continue to be impressed with the growing commitment of our Distributed Leadership Team members and the positive influence they have had on our building. Personally, I am beginning to feel more and more comfortable in "distributing" leadership opportunities to team members and other teacher leaders in our building. Team members and teacher leaders are also feeling more comfortable in "stepping up to the plate," and taking responsibility for many activities and functions in our building.

It was our plan to optimally customize our work in the schools while developing a teacher leader development program that was transportable to sites that wished to engage in building DL teams and settings. It was our intent to develop teacher leaders who could coach colleagues, support learning communities, and lead instruction-based issues (data analysis and planning, staff development, retraining staff, curriculum and instruction planning, etc.) in their buildings.

Instructional Design and Modifications

All modules were instructionally designed by the School District of Philadelphia and the University of Pennsylvania, and consisted of a facilitator guidebook, participant guidebook, PowerPoint synopsis, and a videotape of the original presenter. The instructional designer was a

Newfoundland company, KLi: Advanced Distributed Learning for a New World, who proposed and assumed the design to be a blend of 25 minutes of presentation, 25 minutes of discussion, and 10 minutes of exercises per hour. The presentation focused on the instructor's presentation of essential, knowledge-based informational content; the discussion enabled learners to demonstrate understanding of the content through Q and A sessions and group discussions; and exercises included, but were not limited to, problem-solving, which proved the most engaging and required the greatest degree of critical thinking. Videos were edited to be consistent with the instructional design of the modules. As we entered high schools (years two and three), we found sessions focused on trust building, change strategies, and networks to be useful to practitioners.

Participants rated modules as highly successful and meaningful (4.8 average on a 5.0 scale). The training became an important source of skill sets that teams focused on and used in their early teamwork and routines. For example, the module that focused on data analysis and use became the stimulus to develop data walls, to better display and utilize student data for instruction. By year three of the project, most schools had developed and were using data walls systematically at the building level. Other teams benefited from the cognitive psychology in the team-building and conflict-resolution modules to influence colleagues in their instructional endeavors. The modules were purposeful in that they developed new competencies and new commitments that led to school reculturing—pulling them away from traditional practice and the assumptions that drive them (Dufour, Eaker, & Dufour, 2005).

This training also benefited the team-building process. The school teams (principal, assistant principal, teacher leaders, and coach) attended training sessions together, and all participated in those activities designed to help teams both know each other and work well together. This became an effective part of our team-building process.

Building-based Training

Given our program logic, it was important that we assisted in the development of a shared vision in each building, and supported the discussion about, and implementation of, effective instructional practices. In an effort to create not only leadership continuity but also a collective capacity to impact student achievement, we complemented our leadership training, and the training the district had already provided to schools, with more building support in the form of team-initiated training. This would assist in ensuring continuity spread widely across building faculty. As a result, 40 hours of building-determined, need-specific supplemental training that might be required, in order to address either curricula or instruction issues, was intended as part of this project, and was provided in support of the district's standards and program objectives.

To support this important element of the project, a distinguished program in Penn's Graduate School of Education, The Penn Literacy Network (PLN), was involved. Led by Dr. Bonnie Botel-Sheppard, PLN has enjoyed a twenty-six-year history in providing long-term, comprehensive, self-sustaining professional development and coaching in literacy and mathematics best practices, to districts across several states. PLN completed an on-site assessment of literacy and numeracy practices to ascertain if these districts were rich in active reading, writing, speaking, and listening activities that promote critical thinking, problem-solving, and logical reasoning, as focused on the Pennsylvania Academic Standards and the District's curricula. They helped to evaluate existence of a shared vision and best practices in each building.

The results of this assessment identified deficits in virtually all of our sites, and helped to determine what additional training or coaching was necessary in literacy and numeracy in each building. The faculty and leadership team in each school developed a plan based on this work. The project has involved PLN and other specific consultants in targeted follow-ups. This has been an important prerequisite concurrent with the development of professional learning communities. One first project principal describes the impact of this professional development on her personal growth and the professional learning community (PLC) in her building:

> My significant growth has been in two areas. First, I am becoming more familiar with how a quality PLC should work. Second, I am working on school-wide improvement on writing skills. I am reading and researching more on what good writing looks like. I have learned where I want to begin in September with writing skills across all grade levels. I have not been satisfied with the

writing I have seen in some grade levels, and in some specific areas of the curriculum. It is time to do something about it. The DL Program has supported this with high-quality PD [professional development] . . . It inspired me, as well as inspired most of the faculty members to step up their game. After that PD I miss having my own classroom where I could share and try some of the things that were presented.

We would note that the 40 hours of building-level development made a substantial difference, for several reasons. First, as leadership changed in the district, professional development for building staff diminished. As stated earlier, our professional development was the only source for teachers to address their needs. Second, developing teacher leaders and leadership teams in poorly resourced and poorly functioning school systems, without providing an alternative to address deficits and needs, only frustrated teacher leaders ready to move forward. Third, the very act of choice and autonomy in addressing needs was an important use of the leadership skills developed, and it provided leadership opportunities. The Project Director believed, and our experience in two projects confirmed, that this building-based training was an important source of autonomy and choice that motivated teacher leaders and their colleagues, especially in poor urban schools. The fact that they had resources for resolving their identified needs empowered them in the building to attack even problems they needed support for, as well as those that they could address directly. This enhanced their credibility and the perception that they were truly teacher "leaders."

One principal in the second project explained the impact of building professional development in his school:

The DL Program has contributed greatly to our instructional program, and our DL team has earned the respect and trust of the entire faculty. DL teachers lead by designing PD that has faculty input, and addresses faculty needs, interacting and collaborating with individuals and departments on improving instruction, and completing goals on their action plans. If it wasn't for the DL Program, we might not have technology in our school—at least for our students.

One principal from the first project commented on how the training and coaching affected her:

> I think about how I have grown so much as a leader. Of course I wish that I knew eight years ago what I know now to guide my professional practice. Unfortunately, it doesn't happen that way. The DL training gave me a road map as a structure to help me develop into a more effective leader, of which I am very proud. The PD and weekly coaching was most valuable . . .

Another described the impact of the training on her school:

> What a great year! The DL team led, or was part of all initiatives, and inspired colleagues to actively participate. The DL team also spent time reviewing what worked and what needed to change. So often we continue with an intervention but we don't stop to measure its effectiveness for students. The DL team took that head-on, reviewing data and making changes to student groups.

Leadership Coaching

We trained experienced leadership coaches with our teams (teacher leaders and principals) to build collaboration and fidelity in implementing our training. In their comprehensive study of coaching in America's Choice schools, Poglinco et al. (2003) described coaching as "a form of inquiry-based learning characterized by collaboration between individual, or groups of, teachers and more accomplished peers" (p. 1). They further explain that coaching involves professional, ongoing classroom/team modeling, supportive critiques of practice, and specific observations. The Annenberg Institute (2004) has further stated that "effective coaching encourages collaborative practice" (p. 2), and that the impact of an effective coaching program "can affect the culture of a school" (p. 2). The use of leadership coaches was not a common practice in most efforts to implement distributed leadership.

Neufeld and Roper (2003) in their monograph entitled *Coaching: A strategy for developing instructional capacity,* argue for "change coaching," which addresses "whole school, organizational improvement and helps schools examine their resources—time, money, and personnel – and allocate them more effectively. [Change coaches] developed the leadership skills of both teachers and principals" (pp. 4–6). Neufeld and Roper identify the following ways in which change coaches can help those administrators and teacher leaders:

- Help principals understand the importance of recruiting teachers to assume instructional leadership roles, to drive whole-school change.
- Act as strategists and assistants in building capacity for shared decision-making.
- Model leadership skills for principals, as well as for teachers.
- Assist in scheduling.
- Help principals organize their time so that they are able to visit classrooms regularly to observe instruction and offer feedback to teachers.

Change or leadership coaches (called capacity coaches in the Boston Annenberg site) were extremely valuable in developing a distributed school setting and leadership agenda in such a setting. Also, leadership coaching was consistent with one of Hackman's (2009) five basic conditions to create and maintain effective teams.

For Neufeld and Roper (2003), the goal of coaching is "to engage educators in collaborative work designed to contribute to the development of intellectual capital in schools" (pp. 26f.). It is clear that training itself does not necessarily result in enhanced performance. Hesketh (1997) indicated that one issue in the lack of transfer of training is that, in general, training programs do not impart metacognitive skills explicitly to trainees. Yet metacognitive skills—the ability to think about one's thoughts, feelings, and behaviors—are essential features in mastering new skills (Carver & Scheier, 1998). See Yoak's (2013) dissertation about how DL teacher leaders consider, and come to understand, their own leadership thinking as participants in this process. Since the fostering of metacognitive skills is central to the coaching process, coaching may prove to be a useful adjunct or replacement for some training programs. Olivero, Bane, and Kopelman (1997) found that training, followed by one-to-one coaching, significantly increased productivity compared to training alone. We have endeavored to effect similar results using multiple strategies, including content and capacity coaching.

Since leadership coaching was the primary coaching used in the project, we utilized the knowledge, skills, and experience of retired principals and school leaders, handpicked for their specific skills. After being chosen through a rigorous interview process with the project leaders, all our coaches attended training with the leadership teams, supplemented by sessions with coaches trained in the National Mentor's Center (National Association of Secondary School Principals).

Once trained, these coaches were hired to spend ten hours per week (halved after the first year in the Archdiocese project) in each distributed leadership building, coaching each team and their members. In this way, an ongoing presence could reinforce the leadership skills, action plans, and developments that the teams undertook. They also reinforced the literacy and numeracy practices, and assisted in facilitating the 40 hours of prescribed professional development. The coaches were deeply experienced school and district leaders, with knowledge of change and complex project management. They met regularly with the project leaders and each other, helping to maintain program consistency and implementation, while advising colleagues on challenging issues. Also proving instrumental in sharing successes and best practices across buildings, they are highly valued by the teams, who said:

> Our coach continues to be a strong mentor for our team. We are grateful for having her with us as she understands the education system and her views are always insightful. She is supportive and resourceful. I enjoy meeting with her one-on-one when she visits on non-meeting days.
>
> (Second project high-school principal #1)

> Our coach continues to be a positive influence in the school family. He brings a unique perspective to our DL team and challenges us to think outside the box. We are thankful to him for helping us get a busy consultant to run a PD and providing relevant readings.
>
> (Second project high-school principal #2)

Another school expressed this appreciation for their coach:

> He has gained the respect of the distributed leadership team. He shares his perspective at meetings, which differs from the experience of the DL team members. It is good to have him with us.
>
> (First project high-school principal)

Yet another principal, expressing a high trust level in her DL coach, reported that they work in harmony, and she uses her coach's knowledge and experience to guide her own decision-making.

Operationalizing a Distributed Perspective: Five Essential Elements

This chapter has focused on the heart of operationalizing distributed leadership: leadership training, building-based training, and leadership coaching. One of the program's most significant outcomes, found consistently in both projects to date, is the change it enables in school culture. Obviously, causal relationships cannot be identified but only suggested, as we connect our intents to the results related herein. The project finding, supported by randomized trial results, was that the DL Program increased leadership teams' effectiveness and culture, with six factors statistically significant: trust, collective responsibility, efficacy, influence, satisfaction, and opportunities to learn.

The following list highlights critical design elements that were essential in operationalizing a distributed perspective on leadership, and building the leadership and efficacy of our teacher leaders and others. They are discussed and noted here as guidance to those seeking to do this work in their own schools or districts.

1. Create opportunities for teacher leaders and teams to engage in leadership work.

Harris (2008) observes that the successful distribution of leadership in schools "asks those in formal leadership positions to develop informal leaders [e.g., teacher leaders] and to maximize opportunities to develop

The Leadership Practice Aspect

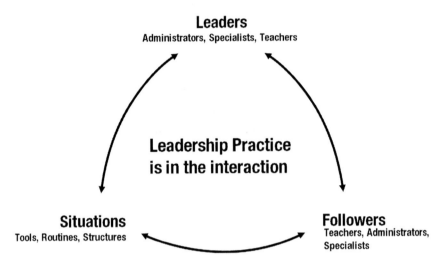

Figure 3.1 Leadership Practice Aspect

Source: Adapted from Spillane, Halverson, & Diamond (2004, p. 11).

their leadership potential" (p. 40). In reflecting on the interplay represented in Figure 3.1, Harris (2008) adds that the successful distribution of leadership in schools "requires those in formal leadership roles to create the cultural and structural conditions or spaces where distributed leadership can operate best and flourish" (p. 40). Such opportunities promote factors impacting efficacy, culture, and team effectiveness.

2. Be flexible enough in your implementation to allow new teacher leaders to choose leadership work that represents one of their strengths.

Gallup research has been with us for many years. Over a decade ago, Gallup surveyed more than 1,000,000 work teams, and conducted over 50,000 in-depth one-on-one interviews. Rath and Conchie (2009) described the results best. When workplace leadership fails to focus on individual strengths, the odds of an employee being engaged are a dismal 1 in 11 (9%), but when strengths are the focus, the odds soar to almost 3 in 4 (73%). The point is, when teacher leaders can focus on multiple tools, routines, and structures to lead in their buildings, doesn't it make sense to at least start with their strengths? This is a critical design element because it affects personal learning and teacher change (Parise & Spillane, 2010). Psychologist Albert Bandura (1977) defined self-efficacy as one's beliefs in one's ability to achieve goals and succeed in specific situations. Zepeda explains that "a self-efficacious person is confident in his/her capacity to achieve goals, to persevere in the face of adversity, and to succeed. In many ways, one's beliefs shape what one considers is possible, which could shape what one pursues—and how" (Zepeda, 2015, p. 6).

Despite several pressures to do otherwise, we were constant in our belief that teacher leaders should choose their early foci for this leadership from their strengths. We encouraged them to examine theirs, and provided the flexibility for early strengths-based choices. This, we believe, helped to foster efficacy, trust, satisfaction, and influence. It also encouraged opportunities to learn.

3. Teach the teams about influence and influence strategies.

We believe several skill sets impact the teacher leaders' early success. The cognitive psychology of influence and influence strategies are established in several modules to add to lessons on leadership. If leadership is viewed from an influence perspective, these skills are essential to the teacher leaders' success. Our feedback from past cohorts has reinforced this belief and the success of this approach, addressing why, as we believe, influence is a cultural element. Influence is also an essential element of James Spillane's definition of distributed leadership: leadership refers to those activities that are either understood by, or designed by, organizational members to influence the motivation, knowledge, affect, and practice of organizational members in the service of the organization's core work (2006, pp. 11–12).

His definition also encouraged us to add another training module, which supports an understanding of influence, but underscores the personal and social skills essential to effective leadership—emotional intelligence (EQ). Since EQ is more predictive of success in a leader than IQ (Goleman, Boyatzis, & McKee, 2002), we included a module on emotional intelligence (developed by Annie McKee's Center in Philadelphia). That module not only supports an understanding of the personal and social skills of influence, but reinforces the willing methods (persuasion, contracts, etc.)

which we believe are more effective in this work and promote satisfaction. One high-school principal assessed the impact of EQ on understanding and influencing leadership this way:

> The DL team continues to conduct effective meetings, and achieve team goals and successful completion of tasks. We have also learned about the emotional intelligence of staff, and the vital role played in understanding that trait. We have tried to learn about each staff member's capacities, increase their enthusiasm and optimism, reduce frustration, and transmit a sense of mission, which we hope will directly increase performance. If we stimulate them intellectually, make available individualized support, and provide them with an appropriate model, we may get more and more leaders.

4. Motivation and trust matter: help them to understand how to create more effective teams and schools.

Colleagues have a role to play in keeping motivation alive in their students and in each other, a topic seldom included either in teacher training or leadership training. Since building trust and knowing how to address trust problems are also seldom taught, we include comprehensive modules on both, and provide an audit tool for motivation, and a trust analysis and agreement for buildings where trust is a problem. Our leaders know how to use them with our support.

We also try to model the principles that Deci et al. (1995 and 2001) and Pink (2009) have urged us to use. Pink, using Deci et al.'s research, believes that to increase motivation and effectiveness, you should zero in on three key elements of current thinking about motivation: autonomy, mastery, and purpose. This research says that, "If you want people to perform at a high level, especially for complicated things, they have to be self-directed, they have to be able to move towards mastery, and they have to have a purpose for what they are doing" (Pink, 2009, pp. 80f.). Supporting autonomy involves providing choices where possible, such as the choice of which routines to begin with. Moving toward mastery involves enhancing competence, so we strive for all of our teacher leaders to gain competence in the target areas they choose. Finally, since purpose is inherent in their targets for their schools and their leadership, we try to meet their needs and create the right conditions for learning and leading. We believe that these efforts have helped to build satisfaction, opportunities to learn trust, and efficacy. Chapter 6 provides a more in-depth discussion of how leadership development dovetails with efforts to build trust in schools.

5. Operationalizing a distributed perspective should focus on teaching and learning.

If this seems obvious, but it is sometimes very difficult and complicated. It is tempting to believe that any setting that is not achieving needs new leadership and more leadership capacity. That may be true, but a setting may also need infrastructure, as discussed in Chapter 2. While we make the assumption that everyone has the basics (coherent curriculum, instructional plans, and authentic literacy and assessments) in place, many do not. So your focus on distributed leadership and building leadership capacity may require parallel paths.

We recommend that you require, or conduct, an educational audit on the condition of teaching and learning, to determine where you stand in the process. Then, you can set realistic goals and your DL teams can realistically support your focus on teaching and learning. Unrealistic goals will frustrate your leadership efforts and your developing teacher leaders. Realistic goals will allow you to determine the timeline, level of skills needed, and the scope of your efforts, while adding realistic purpose to your teams, and motivating them to make a difference in your school.

Chapter Summary

Based on Spillane's seven-year study we developed modules of training designed for greater instructional effectiveness. Building-based training supported the leadership training, and is described as an essential support to the leadership teams. Leadership coaching was an essential strategy for creating and sustaining effective teams. Finally, five essential elements of operationalizing distributed leadership provide guidance for leaders seeking to implement DL in leader development programs or at school sites.

Chapter Discussion Questions

1. What opportunities for teacher leadership exist within your school or district context?
2. How would you operationalize a distributed perspective on leadership and build the leadership and efficacy of your teacher leaders in your school setting?

Suggested Reading

- Boyatzis, R., & McKee, A. (2005). *Resonant leadership*. Boston, MA: Harvard Business School Press.
- Cialdini, R. B. (2009). *Influence: Science and practice*. Boston, MA: Pearson Education.
- Deci, E. L., & Flaste, R. (1995). *Why we do what we do: Understanding self-motivation*. New York, NY: Penguin.
- Pink, D. (2009). *Drive: The surprising truth about what motivates us*. New York, NY: Riverhead.
- Rath, T., & Conchie, B. (2009). *Strength-based leadership: Great leaders, teams, and why people follow*. New York, NY: Gallup Press.

References

Annenberg Institute. (2004). Instructional coaching: A professional development strategy that improves instruction. Brown University, Rhode Island: Annenberg Institute for School Reform, p. 2.

Bandura, A. (1977). Self-efficacy: Toward a unifying theory of behavioral change. *Psychology Review. 84*(2), 191–215.

Carver, C. S., & Scheier, M. F. (1998). *On the self-regulation of behavior*. Cambridge, UK: Cambridge University Press.

Conchie, B., & Rath, T. (2009). *Strengths-based leadership: Great leaders, teams, and why people follow*. New York, NY: Gallup Press.

Deci, E. L., & Flaste, R. (1995). *Why we do what we do: Understanding self-motivation*. New York, NY: Penguin.

Deci, E. L., Koestner, R., & Ryan, R. M. (2001). Extrinsic rewards and intrinsic motivation in education: Reconsidered once again. *Review of Educational Research, 71*(1), 1–27.

Dufour, R., Eaker, R., & Dufour, R. (Eds.). (2005). *On common ground: The power of professional learning communities*. Bloomington, IN: National Educational Service.

Fullan, M. (2001). *Leading in a culture of change*. San Francisco, CA: Jossey-Bass.

Goleman, D., Boyatzis, R., & McKee, A. (2002). *The new leaders: Transforming the art of leadership into the science of results.* London: Time-Warner.

Hackman, J. R. (2009). In D. Coutu, Why teams don't work. *Harvard Business Review, 87*(5), 103.

Harris, A. (2008). *Distributed school leadership: Developing tomorrow's leaders*. London; New York: Routledge.

Hesketh, B. (1997). Dilemmas in training for transfer and retention. *Applied Psychology: An International Review, 46*(4), 317–386.

Neufeld, B., & Roper, D. (2003). *Coaching: A strategy for developing instructional capacity*. Aspen Institute Program on Education: The Annenberg Institute for School Reform.

Olivero, G., Bane, K. D., & Kopelman, R. E. (1997). Executive coaching as a transfer of training tool: Effects on productivity in a public agency. *Public Personnel Management, 26*(4), 461–469.

Parise, L. M. & Spillane, J. P. (2010). Teacher learning and instructional change: How formal and on-the-job learning opportunities predict changes in elementary school teachers' instructional practice. *Elementary School Journal, 110*(3), 323–346.

Pink, D. (2009). *Drive: The surprising truth about what motivates us*. New York, NY: Riverhead.

Poglinco, S., Bach, A., Hovde, K., Rosenblum, S., Saunders, M., & Supovitz, J. (2003). The heart of the matter: The coaching model in America's choice schools. Philadelphia: Consortium for Policy Research in Education,

University of Pennsylvania. Available from: www.cpre.org/ Publication/ Publications_Research.htm. p. 1.

Rath, T., & Conchie, B. (2009). *Strengths based leadership: Great leaders, teams and why people follow.* New York, NY: Gallup Press.

Sergiovanni, T. J. (2001). *Leadership: What's in it for schools?* New York, NY: Routledge-Falmer.

Spillane, J. P. (2006). *Distributed leadership.* San Francisco, CA: Jossey-Bass.

Spillane, J. P. (2008). *The distributed perspective: Module two of the distributed leadership series: Diagnosis and design. Facilitator's guide.* Evanston, IL: The School of Education and Social Policy, Northwestern University.

Spillane, J. P., & Diamond, J. B. (2007). *Distributed leadership in practice.* New York, NY: Teachers College Press.

Spillane, J. P., Halverson, R., & Diamond, J. (2004) Towards a theory of leadership practice: A distributed perspective. *Journal of Curriculum Studies, 36*(1), 3–34. doi:10.1080/0022027032000106726.

Yoak, E. (2013). *Learning for leadership: Understanding adult learning to build school leadership capacity* [Doctoral dissertation]. University of Pennsylvania, Philadelphia. Available from ProQuest Dissertations and Theses database (UMI No. 36–10081).

Zepeda, S. (2015). *Job-embedded professional development: Support, collaboration, and learning in schools.* New York, NY: Routledge.

Distributed Leadership for Building School Leadership Capacity

Part II extends the thematic elements presented in Part I, but with chapters that address more directly how distributed leadership is, and may be operationalized in schools, plus the potential results that can follow. Whereas Part I focused more on distributed leadership (DL) theory, and program design, this part discusses what happened at schools that implemented the curriculum and design presented in Part I. Leveraging the theory and content of the distributed perspective, the DL Program created teacher leadership roles on school-based leadership teams. This restructuring had a strong impact on school culture, giving rise to new norms and routines in support of teacher leadership. Throughout Part II, additional connections are drawn between DL and other theoretical or practical approaches to understanding and building school capacity, including the observation that practitioner learning is a key driver for change in schools. As a whole, this part takes a closer look at what DL looks like in schools, to help practitioners understand the ways in which they may enact this work in their own leadership practice.

Distributed Leadership Teams

A Model for Team Leadership Development and Building Leadership Capacity in Schools

In this chapter . . .

Organizational Leadership in the Twenty-First Century

In 2002, Sheila Webber, citing the *Harvard Business Review* (1994), discussed a trend in organizational leadership: twenty-first century organizations were experiencing a greater prevalence of teams and a concurrent rise in the diverse makeup of such teams. Specifically, twenty-first century teams, "due to changing workforce demographics and the development of new organizational forms," were increasingly comprised of employees from different functional areas in the organization (p. 201). Webber referred to these as *cross-functional teams*.

With regard to Webber's point, organizations are increasingly reliant on teams for organizing the accomplishment of work, and schooling organizations are no exception.[1] Likewise, leadership, whether conceived as influence, a result of personal interaction styles, activity, or otherwise, is indispensable as a driving factor in moving organizational work forward.[2] But while there is much written on team development and leadership, "existing models are limited in their ability to provide prescriptions to guide team leadership and to enhance team development" (Zaccaro, Rittman, & Marks, 2001, p. 452), whether with respect to cross-functional teams or other team forms.

With this concern, the extensive implementation of the Distributed Leadership (DL) Program is instructive for practitioners seeking robust models emphasizing teamwork, team development, and team leadership in their schools. This program provides further insight into how to develop effective leadership teams representing diverse professional functions in schools.

Per the DL Program's structure, the primary vehicle for operationalizing distributed leadership at participating campuses involved the creation of school leadership teams (*i.e.,* "distributed leadership teams" or "DL teams") composed of practitioners pulled from different functional areas in schools (*e.g.,* school administrators, teachers, coaches, supervisors, and more). Because of its particular reliance on team development, the DL Program provides insight and perspective on how cross-functional DL teams can operate effectively in leading improvement efforts in schools.

Table 4.1 Typology of Team Leadership Frameworks

Leadership Framework Type	Description	Suggested Reading
Input	Individual leaders' characteristics or attributes that influence, guide, and structure team experiences and productivity.	*Kozlowski, Gully, Salas, & Cannon-Bowers (1996)* Discussing how to train individual leaders for leading/directing teams.
		Bass (1990); Avolio & Bass (1999) Discussing transformational and transactional leadership styles; how individuals share vision with employees; discussing task and relational roles for individual leaders.
Output	Leadership as an outcome of team activity.	*Day, Gronn, & Salas (2004)* Discussing the input-process-output (I-P-O) and the input-mediator-output-input (I-M-O-I) frameworks, whereby an example of an output of team leadership can include team performance (e.g., student achievement, accomplishment of objective(s), etc.).
Emergent	Leadership as a process, emerging from within a team; as a product of collective activity; and/or leadership as interaction.	*Gronn (2000); Day, Gronn, & Salas (2004); Spillane (2006)* Discussing the *how* of leadership; leadership as an activity, emerging from the interaction between leaders and followers (identified by specific role in a situation rather than by title and formal role); shaped by applicable organizational structures and routines
	Also may include leadership as resulting from multiple individuals enacting specific leadership behaviors contemporaneously.	*Sivasubramanian, Murry, Avolio, & Jung (2002)* Distinguishing between team leadership and individual leadership; discussing team leadership as the collective influence of team members on each other.

(continued)

Table 4.1 (continued)

Leadership Framework Type	Description	Suggested Reading
Synergistic	Leadership capacity; leadership as social capital, as capitalized through reciprocal interactions/exchanges; leadership as a result of social network activity, where human interaction produces group capacity that, on the whole, is greater than the sum of individual capacities on a team.	*Gronn (2002); Zaccaro, Rittman, & Marks (2001)* Discussing reciprocal or collective influence as a type of "conjoint agency" or "synergy," whereby each unit member influences each other unit member in successive phases of interaction; the result is pooled, distributed capacity.
Integrated	Leadership and team processes as inextricably integrated; fairly indistinct.	*Zaccaro & Klimoski (2002)* Discussing the "interface" between leadership and team processes noting the potential for indistinctness between the same; fundamental integration between team and leadership processes.

What is Team Leadership?

Rather than being characterized by a single concept or type of practice, team leadership can refer to multiple, complex, and varied practices, events, or phenomena. Table 4.1 lists different examples of how team leadership has been defined in educational research.

The list in Table 4.1 elucidates the following observation: team leadership can entail a diversity of approaches. It is, thus, important that practitioners seeking to develop or enhance team leadership in their schools acquaint themselves with how the practice of team leadership can vary, and also, how it can be analyzed and better understood across perspectives.

Indeed, the DL Program implementation of DL teams could be discussed using several of the frameworks listed in Table 4.1. Also, note that while Table 4.1 may portray various leadership types as more or less distinct, there is certainly much overlap and relationship between the types of leadership detailed above.

For example, while the categories of leadership described as *output* or *emergent* types emphasize product and process elements, separately and respectively, *synergistic* leadership blurs the distinction between product and process, blending these elements in a nuanced but related definition of team leadership.

The synergistic leadership framework, which presents an understanding of leadership as both process *and* product, is underscored in the following vignette because it is particularly useful in identifying the conditions and processes enacted to develop team leadership capacity in schools through DL teams.

Distributed Leadership/Synergistic Leadership Vignette

Principal Jones, in his first year at Wayside Middle School, decides to implement distributed leadership (DL). Mr. Jones discusses this course of action with the greater faculty and asks for volunteers to submit a brief application form to serve on the school's new DL team.

(continued)

(continued)

To select team members, Principal Jones works with the central administrative office to provide third-party reviewers of teacher applications, and to make selections objectively. Once decisions are made, selected teachers are informed and the team holds its first meeting.

At the meeting, Ms. Mitchell addressed the team. "I would like to talk about what has been bothering many teachers on campus since the departure of our last campus principal," she said. Ms. Mitchell had been one of the top-scoring candidates by third-party reviewers of DL team applicants. "Teachers at Wayside Middle School have felt ignored," she said, "and their suggestions for instructional improvement disregarded. We would appreciate the opportunity to visit with our campus departments and fellow faculty, to determine what they believe are the most pressing needs facing our campus. I believe that if we were to develop an action plan agenda based on teachers' analysis and suggestions, we would generate greater faculty support and lay the foundation for this team's success at Wayside."

Mr. Jones reflected: the teachers selected for the DL team clearly had more knowledge than he on how other faculty in the building felt. Hearing the voices of other faculty would begin with him hearing the faculty voices right in front of him.

Principal Jones observed other DL team members, Ms. Ginny, Mr. Parker, and Ms. Simone, nodding their heads in agreement with Ms. Mitchell's comments. Mr. Parker added, "Campus morale was deeply affected by the often imposing policies of the previous school administrator. It would be helpful if this team can be more than just another reform effort. We have an opportunity to lead Wayside in a new direction, one that shows other teachers that they are being listened to."

In response to the teachers' comments, Mr. Jones proposed that the DL team teachers co-lead the upcoming faculty meeting to elicit responses, and identify areas for strategic reform by and with faculty colleagues. On the group's consensus, Ms. Mitchell proposed the team's strategy for data collection and action plan development going forward. The Wayside Middle School DL team was born.

The above vignette captures how relational exchanges can produce synergy and new direction for a campus. Although Principal Jones initiated implementation of DL at his school, the teachers on the team quickly proved themselves to be invaluable resources and repositories of influence among the greater faculty. What began as a principal-led initiative developed into a team-led initiative the moment the principal and teacher leaders at Wayside charted a course for instructional improvement together. It is likely as difficult for principals to sit back and listen to faculty proposals as it may be for faculty to step up and usher such proposals. Mr. Jones' willingness to move away from a principal-crafted agenda and listen to and abide by a team consensus was a shift away from the campus norm established by his predecessor, and ensured a new direction for Wayside.

Building Leadership Capacity in Schools: Distributed Leadership Teams as a Tool for Restructuring and Reculturing Schools

Introducing DL teams as a new structure in schools can promote leadership capacity, and can prove to be a significant structural factor driving improvement initiatives. DL teams facilitate improvement efforts in schools by *restructuring* the interactive modes through which work gets done. Through DL teams, new leadership and organizational activity can be initiated and coordinated: teacher-administrative teaming, teacher-led faculty trainings/professional development, collective data gathering and analysis, team action planning, and more.

But restructuring alone is not enough. Fullan (2001) writes that "structure does make a difference, but it is not the main point in achieving success. Transforming the culture—changing the way we do things around here—is the main point" (pp. 43f.). Thus, in addition to structure, processes of *reculturing* (*i.e.,* enculturation of norms of trust, collaboration, and innovation and team leadership culture), as Fullan terms it, are critical in leading school improvement.

Figure 4.1 portrays how DL team leadership structures in schools can give rise to new routines, practices, and cultural norms that then influence the team's other leadership structures, reciprocally, which again modify

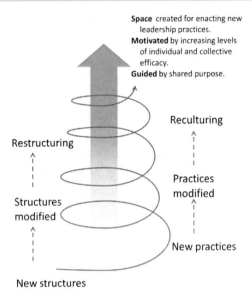

Space created for enacting new leadership practices.
Motivated by increasing levels of individual and collective efficacy.
Guided by shared purpose.

Reculturing

Restructuring

Practices modified

Structures modified

New practices

New structures

Figure 4.1 Relationship between Restructuring and Reculturing Processes in Developing Leadership Capacity

Source: Abdul-Jabbar & Yoak, 2012.

practices, and so on. The figure models the interrelationship between restructuring and reculturing processes in developing leadership capacity in organizations.

The descriptive analysis presented in the following section exemplifies how such change unfolded across campuses participating in the DL Program (including elementary and secondary schools). The section depicts processes by which recently implemented DL teams influenced the growth in leadership capacity at their schools, and is instructive for intervention models or approaches seeking to promote leadership capacity in schools, by implementing similar leadership team structures.

A Descriptive Analysis of the Impact of DL Teams on Leadership Capacity at Participating Schools

An effective leadership team culture encouraged the active soliciting of input from team members, and promoted team meetings as a dialogical space rather than as rigidly hierarchical. The DL team structure at one participating school, St. Ivy,[3] incubated teacher leadership in the school through introducing new roles for teacher and administrator participants, and new norms of group collaboration and interaction (e.g., equality, collegiality, and co-leadership). The new leadership culture shifted individual behavior and called team participants to modify their practices. For example, teacher leaders from the DL team developed their own action plans for campus-wide instructional improvement (or for targeted improvement within their respective academies), increasingly led faculty meetings, and codeveloped professional development for their peers. As a result, St. Ivy experienced a growth in teacher-led professional inquiry, in the sharing of instructional strategies, and in the development of new team routines that affected the greater faculty. These outcomes are captured by the Distributed Leadership Program Logic Model (see Chapter 2) as "DL Team Outcomes," and a means for enhancing "School Leadership Capacity." Such effects were observed across implementations of the DL Program and in replications of the same.

Having DL team teachers take the helm in leading action plans, heading faculty meetings and professional development trainings, and conducting surveys and other data collection and analysis projects in their schools produced a noticeable shift towards active teacher participation, involvement, and engagement.

At St. Ivy, the DL team's influence spread through restructured faculty meetings (an action plan initiative proposed and implemented by the teacher participants on the team), which saw a concurrent rise in the development of new routines supporting the diffusion of such influence. Team leadership became anchored more readily in the structure and culture of the school. As team members grew more receptive to being influenced by one another, and as the faculty grew more receptive to being influenced by the DL team (i.e., via ongoing implementation and active monitoring of action plans and the like), the school's leadership capacity noticeably increased.

Staff exchanges were dynamic and mission-related, and opportunities for faculty feedback increased. A healthy culture of risk-taking and initiative emerged amongst DL team members, as did an increasing orientation to innovation, adaptation, and teacher leadership.

At another participating school, the principal shared how she had always sought to cultivate shared decision-making norms with her teachers, yet had lacked the means and structure to do so. Implementation of the DL Program at her school enabled her team to confront this challenge, expanding their definition(s) of leadership while broadening their awareness of more diverse applications for teacher agency. Addressing the shift in the decision-making culture, norms, and routines on her campus, she explained:

> Sure. I think the teachers, the faculty themselves were used to having someone from administration lead meetings . . . Well, I think it's one of the things we've been working on for a very long time. I think the nature of schools is such that teachers just expect administrators to make decisions and they're kind of either victim of it or happy because of it. Since I became principal six years ago we've really worked at shared decision-making . . . [Distributed leadership] fit right in and it kind of validated what we were doing and helped to give us more skill and knowledge to enhance it.
>
> (Catherine, personal interview, June 4, 2012)

Decision-making norms that require *group consensus* (*i.e.*, from teachers and principals in active collaboration) helped to foster collegiality and the valuing of others' opinions. For example, in one interview, a principal, describing how her working relationship with her DL team teachers had evolved, said:

> I think it's become more collegial in that we've learned to work together really well . . . we look at each other more as peers. They're not looking at me as the leader, principal, or boss, and working together in a good way has spilled over to many, not all, but many of the other faculty members. I've seen them step up and say, 'I'll help do that.' or 'Can I do this?' in a way that maybe they wouldn't, or hadn't, done before.
>
> (Beverly, personal interview, June 4, 2012)

The DL Program enabled teachers and principals to regard one another as professional peers and co-equals. This effect was the outcome of team-developed vision and mission foci that were later instantiated in collaboratively developed team action plans, implemented and monitored by all DL team members. These action plans, by focusing and guiding team energies over the course of leading a particular change effort, contributed to team efficiency and organizational leadership capacity.

Ten years of program development and implementation, including redesign and replication of the DL Program, helped us identify key principles which may inform similar efforts seeking to lead school improvement.

As detailed in Chapter 2, the key elements of the DL Program driving the restructuring and reculturing efforts in participating schools included the following:

1. Leadership teams that provided a collaborative planning space for principals and teacher leaders to codevelop action-planning initiatives;

2. Extensive professional development for leadership team members;

3. Supplemental building-based training and, when applicable, in-house professional development for remaining staff; and

4. Leadership team coaching and ongoing support.

These programmatic elements, included in the design, redesign, and replication of the DL Program, are program staples. See Part I for more in-depth discussion of the program's operationalization.

Caveat on Incentive Pay

One caveat to the above description and analysis is the observation that incentive pay, even if nominal, may influence results. During the course of project implementation in the Archdiocese, for example, when funding was interrupted to teachers, there was a concurrent retraction in teacher effort and motivation at some schools. We do not believe that this suggests that incentive pay is a necessary component in sustaining or even initiating the type of growth in capacity depicted and portrayed in Figure 4.1. It is more likely that when one creates a structure with a monetary incentive built in, this fact impacts the school culture, too. When monetary incentives once provided are suspended, it can feel like punishment or a lack of commitment by organizers. It is not unusual, then, that money as an incentive, when no longer provided, can create exactly the opposite effects in schools (i.e., decrease in leadership capacity, motivation, etc.), as it did when an intervention was working well.

Further, "there is extensive evidence that teachers regard professional efficacy, not money, as the primary motivator in their work, and some evidence that the prospect of extrinsic rewards may diminish the potency of intrinsic rewards for them" (Johnson, 1986, p. 55). This is an important point for intervention programs that incorporate or seek to incorporate incentive pay.

Comparing Cross-functional, Distributed Leadership Teams and Professional Learning Communities

There is much overlap between DL teams, as a team structure in schools, and *professional learning communities* (PLCs), another team-oriented structure, widely implemented in schools. The DL Program curriculum focused on PLC development as an essential element in the training and professional development of school leadership teams and as important in growing leadership capacity (see Table 3.1, Module 2). But DL teams and PLCs are distinct. A brief comparison here between the two types of strategic, team-focused implementations may prove fruitful for practitioners more familiar with one or the other rather than both.

Eaker, DuFour, and DuFour (2002) describe the conceptual framework of PLCs as subject to three major themes. In their description, PLCs entail: (1) a solid foundation consisting of collaboratively developed and widely shared mission, vision, values, and goals; (2) collaborative teams that work interdependently to achieve common goals; and (3) a focus on results, as evidenced by a commitment to continuous improvement (p. 3). Based on this description, practitioners familiar with PLC research and implementation may find that development of campus DL teams closely parallels the development of PLCs, in that each DL team is similarly constituted by collaborative groupings, and furthermore, that the intention behind the establishment of each team was that its members act in concert, to design and implement continuous instructional improvement in their schools.

A notable difference between the two models includes the observation that DL teams, as conceived in the DL Program, emphasize cross-functional team assignments (*i.e.*, principals, teachers and coaches are represented on every DL team), while PLCs may entail teams that are functionally homogeneous. The two types of structures differ further in that DL teams have the ambition and primary purpose to enact leadership, while PLCs describe teams whose primary activity is to facilitate professional development and collegial learning experiences. Due to an emphasis on learning, PLCs do not typically underscore specific tools and strategies to guide leadership development, although there certainly may be exceptions. In contrast, the DL team experience emphasizes both leading *and* learning, where collaborative learning experiences are an integral part of DL team activity. It is an extension of, and a precursor to, leadership development in the program.

As per the structure of the DL Program, participants were to attend and coparticipate in seventy-seven intensive hours of professional development and co-learning, promote their shared school vision, and coach the greater faculty and staff in its implementation (DeFlaminis, 2011, pp. 39 and 59). It follows that the DL Program's implementation results offer a perspective not only on how teams of professionals in schools lead, but also on how they learn, and more pointedly, *how they learn to lead.* Figures 4.2 and 4.3 suggest two views on how to think about PLC and DL team implementation in schools.

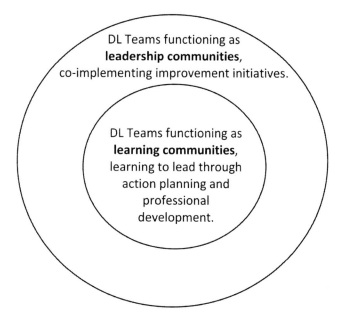

Figure 4.2 A View on DL Team Activity as Both Learning and Leading

Figure 4.2 presents a concentric display wherein the inner circle presents a view of DL team activity, featuring learning as a core activity of team-member interaction. The outer circle reveals an extension of practitioner learning into the practice domain as teachers and principals co-lead, implementing action plans and guiding school improvement. Based on the figure, the "L" in "DL team" could represent both *learning* and *leading*, since both activities are integral to the DL team experience.

At every stage of our implementation, successful DL teams presented as cross-functional, heterogeneous, professional communities, where members learned collaboratively to respect, listen to, and trust one another; to enact policy together; and to lead the greater faculty in similar reculturing processes. Teachers' sense of purpose, motivation, and efficacy were influenced (see Bandura, 1977), as DL team teachers grew to believe that they could make a difference on their campuses.

Figure 4.3 summarizes the abovementioned, and displays how DL teams may provide engineers of school improvement with a concurrent focus on learning and leadership, in a way that capitalizes on the advantages of practitioner learning and leading activity. Both Figures 4.2 and 4.3 reveal that DL teams and PLCs, as team-focused interventions in schools, are quite similar. But there are appreciable differences.

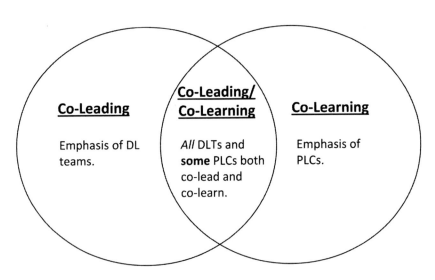

Figure 4.3 A Comparative View on the Purposes and Activities of
DL Teams and PLCs

Table 4.2 presents differences between DL teams and PLCs in a slightly different format than the figures above. The table clarifies whether a particular emphasis is driven by a product or process orientation, and the extent to which homogeneity or heterogeneity is an intended aspect of team design.

DL teams use learning as a lever for leadership development. The learning entails a leadership curriculum (see Chapter 3), and makes use of teachers' energies in guiding action plan codevelopment and implementation. Chapter 5 offers more in-depth discussion on how practitioner learning emerged in the DL Program.

Chapter Summary

School organizations can benefit from improvement planning that emphasizes cross-functional, team experiences, where practitioners both learn and lead together. The DL Program offers an extensive team-leadership design framework for guiding systemic improvement planning in schools, plus a perspective on leadership development that is strengthened by the following observation: the practice of twenty-first-century organizational leadership requires attention to, and an ability to design for, cross-functional, professional leadership teams. To this end, the DL Program incubated heterogeneous leadership teams (*i.e.*, comprised of diverse professional functions), and crafted an instructional curriculum for their professional learning and development, as well as the promotion of leadership capacity in schools. The lessons learned in the DL Program may inform strategic efforts to grow team leadership in school organizations.

Table 4.2 clarifies whether a particular emphasis is driven by a product or process orientation, and the extent to which homogeneity or heterogeneity is an intended aspect of team design.

Table 4.2 Comparing Approaches to Collaborative Leading and Learning in Teams

Change Variable	Distributed Leadership Teams	Professional Learning Communities
Learning	Learning as process/method for training leaders.	Learning as the product/outcome for teams.
Leadership	Leadership as the product/outcome of cross-functional team-member interactions.	Leadership may emerge, incidentally, from teams which may or may not be cross-functional.

Chapter Discussion Questions

1. How do DL teams use learning to build leadership capacity?

2. Think about a change (or reform) that you have created or witnessed that: (a) restructured your school or district; (b) recultured your school or district; or (c) restructured *and* recultured your school or district. Did this change build capacity? If so, how? And how do you know capacity was built?

3. How can a school or district leader use restructuring efforts to facilitate reculturing in school(s)? Can a school or district be recultured without any restructuring effort? Explain.

Suggested Reading

*   Day, D., Gronn, P., & Salas, E. (2004). Leadership capacity in teams. *The Leadership Quarterly, 15*, 857–880.

*   Gronn, P. (2000). Distributed properties: A new architecture for leadership. *Educational Management & Administration, 28*(3), 317–338.

*   Spillane, J. (2006). *Distributed leadership*. San Francisco, CA: Jossey-Bass.

*   Zaccaro, S., & Klimoski, R. (2002). The interface of leadership and team processes. *Group and Organizational Management, 27*, 4–13.

*   Zaccaro, S., Rittman, A., & Marks, M. (2001). Team leadership. *The Leadership Quarterly, 12*, 451–483.

Notes

1. See Day, Gronn, and Salas (2004) explaining that schooling organizations are increasingly dependent on teams.

2. See Bass, 1990; Avolio and Bass, 1999 (discussing leadership as influence); Lewin and Lippit, 1938 (discussing personal leadership styles, individual

leader characteristics/attributes); and Spillane, 2006, 2009 (discussing leadership as activity).

3. "St. Ivy" is a fictitious alias de-identifying an actual school and its research participants to protect the identities and privacy of individuals who participated in our school leadership research and program implementation. The St. Ivy example is offered here due to the relatively large growth in relational/cultural confidence observed across pre/post interviews and surveys conducted at the school. The growth in relational trust and increase in social capital, a topic discussed in Chapter 6, likewise makes the school a prominent example of how *reculturing* processes operate in schools via DL teams.

References

Abdul-Jabbar, M., & Yoak, E. (2012). Learning to trust, learning to lead: Implications for leadership development and building relational trust in schools from the study of a leadership development program. Paper presented at University Council for Educational Administration Annual Convention. Denver, CO.

Avolio, B. J., & Bass, B. M. (1999). Re-examining the components of transformational and transactional leadership using the Multifactor Leadership Questionnaire. *Journal of Occupational Psychology, 72*, 441–462.

Bandura, A. (1977). Self-efficacy: Toward a unifying theory of behavioral change. *Psychological Review, 84*(2), 191–215.

Bass, B. M. (1990). From transactional to transformational leadership: Learning to share the vision. *Organizational Dynamics, 18*(3), 19–31.

Day, D., Gronn, P., & Salas, E. (2004). Leadership capacity in teams. *The Leadership Quarterly, 15*, 857–880.

DeFlaminis, J. A. (2011). The design and implementation of the Annenberg Distributed Leadership Project. Paper presented at the annual meeting of the American Educational Research Association, New Orleans, LA.

Eaker, R., DuFour, R., & DuFour, R. (2002). *Getting started: Reculturing schools to become professional learning communities.* Bloomington, IN: Solution Tree Press.

Elmore, R. F. (2000). *Building a new structure for school leadership. American Educator.* Washington, DC: Albert Shanker Institute.

Fullan, M. (2001). *Leading in a culture of change.* San Francisco, CA: Jossey-Bass.

Gronn, P. (2000). Distributed properties: A new architecture for leadership. *Educational Management & Administration, 28*(3), 317–338.

Gronn, P. (2002). Distributed leadership as a unit of analysis. *The Leadership Quarterly, 13*(4), 423–451.

Johnson, S. M. (1986). Incentives for teachers: What motivates, what matters. *Education Administration Quarteryly, 22*(3), 54–79.

Kozlowski, S., Gully, S., Salas, E., & Cannon-Bowers, J. (1996). Team leadership and development: Theory, principles, and guildlines for training leaders and teams. *Advances in Interdisciplinary Studies of Work Teams, 3,* 253–291.

Sivasubramanian, N., Murry, W., Avolio, B., & Jung, D. (2002). A longitudinal model of the effects of team leadership and group potency on group perfomance. *Group & Organizational Management, 27,* 66–96.

Spillane, J. (2006). *Distributed leadership.* San Francisco, CA: Jossey-Bass.

Webber, S. (2002). Leadership and trust facilitating cross-functional team success. *The Journal of Management Development, 21,* 207–214.

Zaccaro, S., & Klimoski, R. (2002). The interface of leadership and team processes. *Group and Organizational Management, 27,* 4–13.

Zaccaro, S., Rittman, A., & Marks, M. (2001). Team leadership. *The Leadership Quarterly, 12,* 451–483.

Scaling Leadership in Schools

The Development of Teacher Leadership Practice in Distributed Leadership Schools

In this chapter . . .

Introduction

Teacher leadership was a key component of the DL Program. As a vehicle to operationalize DL theory, the program created new roles for teacher leaders and new structures in the form of school-based leadership teams.

These leadership teams were comprised of both teacher leaders and administrators, who collaborated to lead instructional improvements particular to each school's needs and capacities.

Teacher leadership is no longer a new idea in education. It has been well established as a way to disrupt the traditionally flat hierarchy of schools, and heralded as a strategy for keeping highly qualified and motivated teachers in the classroom. By offering expanded opportunities for professional growth, teacher leadership may support efforts to recruit, retain, and develop the best teachers and mitigate teacher turnover.

The education field is complicated, however, by the variety of models for how teacher leadership actually takes shape in practice. Teacher-leadership roles may be negotiated at the school, district, or national level. They may be formal or informal, paid or unpaid. Teachers may be appointed by the principal, elected by staff members, or they can apply through an outside agency. New candidates may be identified annually or as soon as a new need arises. Or teacher leaders may serve in their roles indefinitely. The discrepancies between various models of teacher leadership have made attempts to clearly identify the benefits of teacher leadership, and to provide guidance on best practices, more difficult.

Many research efforts have focused simply on understanding if and how teacher leadership impacts instruction. We have lost sight of an important question, particularly at the school level: How do we develop effective teacher leaders in schools? The DL Program provides a unique opportunity to study how teacher leaders develop into their roles, and how this development is contingent on school context, including the role of the principal. In the DL Program, we look closely at the individual and collective learning which teacher leaders and principals experience as they come to embrace these new roles and structures in their schools.

Understanding practitioners' learning processes is instructive because it can inform how one might: (1) tailor the selection and training of leaders when culturing team leadership structures and processes in schools; (2) provide coaching and support to staff and team members currently undergoing such an implementation; and (3) facilitate team leadership opportunities and experiences that promote staff competencies and habitudes disposed to effecting improvement changes in schools.

This chapter will address how both teacher leaders and the administrators with whom they worked experienced the change processes associated with implementing the DL Program (*i.e.,* creating new roles, learning new routines, and leading instructional innovation). In so doing, we hope to offer lessons from the field for practitioners seeking to grow leadership capacity in their schools, by employing teacher leadership as a lever for change.

Teacher Leader Learning as Transformation

The leadership component of teacher leadership is commonly viewed as an extension of the teaching role. Teacher leaders are selected because they are expert pedagogues in the classroom. As leaders they then work to translate their own instructional expertise into a resource they can share with others. Becoming a leader is thus associated mainly with assuming new tasks and responsibilities, primarily in supporting colleagues' professional learning.

In contrast to this characterization, many DL participants described teacher leadership as a "transformational" experience. Rather than merely acquiring new skills or extending past roles, teacher leaders found themselves to be deeply changed. This impacted how teachers and administrators alike thought of themselves, how they understood *what* leadership was, and informed their approach and strategy in effectuating leadership in their schools. In this way, transformational learning *within* was found to be tied to systemic, institutional change *without*. Furthermore, where transformational learning did not occur, it was often found to represent a barrier to more enhanced leadership practices, thus indicating that transformational learning among staff may be required before organizational change can follow.

Unsurprisingly, certain schools today may require deep change to realize student performance and instructional improvement. Understanding *how* such change can be realized through team leadership processes can inform ongoing and future school improvement efforts. To this end, lessons learned from the DL Program suggest that, as a starting point for improvement planning, deep structural and/or cultural change in schools begins with transformative teacher learning.

First-order and Second-order Change

All learning represents change. But participants in the DL Program repeatedly used the language of transformation to distinguish the kind of learning they were experiencing in the program from other learning experiences. Thus, these representations draw a distinction between the notions of extending current capabilities and roles and transforming relationships and practices. This dichotomy maps the concepts of first- and second-order change.

Learning which accomplishes first-order change within an organization is not transformative; it is accretive. It extends old knowledge and expertise, and is often slow, gradual, and confined to a particular mode of execution or way of doing things. For this reason, first-order change rarely shifts culture, and in instances where more fundamental cultural/systemic shift is needed, the failure to achieve a second-order change can explain why some improvement efforts fall short of expectations. But first-order change may be appropriate where the task does not require systemic overhaul. Knowing when and where first- or second-order change is needed can promote greater organizational competence, as leaders learn to tailor improvement efforts to organizational needs.

One way of thinking about first-order change is that while change happens, it unfolds within currently established boundaries (Watzlawick, Weakland, & Fisch, 1974), not across them. For example, several theories of how adults learn in schools portray teacher leadership as primarily the acquisition of new responsibilities or skills; participants in learning are viewed as passive receptacles for knowledge deposited into their minds. This reflects a "banking concept" of education (Freire, 1970). New ideas are simply deposited into our minds like money added to a bank vault. Many faculty meetings which feature administrators talking to faculty at length, with little faculty input or exchange, model the banking concept of education. As a change process, this model presents a kind of learning that may be classified as first-order.

In contrast to a banking concept of learning, which features passive roles for teachers, transformational or transformative learning is accompanied by "a deep, structural shift in basic premises of thought, feelings, and actions" (Transformative Learning Centre, 2014). It may be classified as second-order change: that change which explicitly changes *a system* itself

Table 5.1 First- and Second-Order Change

First-order change	Second-order change
• Change within the confines of an existing system or framework of thought and action. • Change which primarily enhances or extends existing thinking or practice.	• Change which changes the system itself. • Change which transforms relationships among thoughts, actions, and perceptions.

and not just the components within the system. Unlike passive, acquisition learning, which occurs within existing boundaries, transformational learning redraws the map.

This distinction is captured by Table 5.1, which contrasts first-order and second-order change.

In understanding *how* the DL Program's approach and strategy can build leadership capacity in schools, we draw on the ideas of second-order change and transformation, in order to understand how the learning experiences of teacher leaders and principals informed reculturing shifts discussed in the previous chapter. Particularly, we will look at which systems were transformed through their participation in the program, and how the DL Program provided a mechanism for this change.

Chapter 8 also presents an extended discussion on tips, tools, and strategies that, among other things, offers prescriptive considerations for nurturing and evaluating first- and second-order change in schools, through stimulating practitioner learning and identity development.

Transformation as the Disruption of Past Norms

The DL Program, and the creation of teacher-leadership roles specifically, disrupted past norms of thinking and practice at many schools. As discussed in Chapter 1, most participants' pre-DL notions of leadership were influenced by hierarchical or top-down leadership approaches, which looked at leadership as primarily the province of formal leaders (e.g., administrators). While teacher leadership roles are, in their own way, a formalization of potentially more organic forms of leadership as enacted by teachers and others in the school community, the creation of these roles between administrators and teachers began to broaden participants' notions of who leads, and what counts as leadership. In many schools, teacher-leadership roles became a gateway, redefining and expanding access to leadership activity for other members of the school community.

In the context of the DL Program, teacher leaders did not passively receive new ideas about leadership, but actively applied what they learned. They took up new ways of thinking about leadership in relationship to their practice, such that changes in thinking and practice were linked and mutually reinforcing. Studying participants' stories of change revealed how their support for, or enactment of teacher-leadership roles implicated multiple aspects of their professional identity.

All schools have a mechanism for leader-identity development, often a result of school or district leadership culture. Even where there is no explicit mechanism in place, leader identity emerges in the context of the roles, behaviors, and frameworks for defining, practicing, and understanding leadership activity in a particular school or district community.

Figure 5.1 depicts a system of leader-identity development, whose three components—leadership roles, leadership behaviors, and leadership frameworks—function as a system of leadership thought and action, which gives rise to leader-identity development.[1]

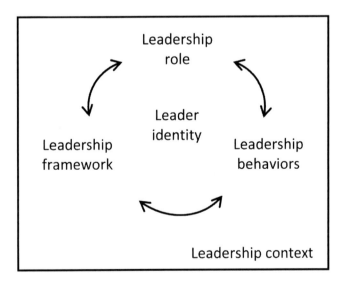

Figure 5.1 Model of Leader Identity in the DL Program

Not all learning reaches participants' identities. The results of the DL Program, in influencing how participants saw themselves, demonstrate that learning can be a powerful change variable for school improvement, impacting not only what practitioners do, but also reshaping who they are, how they see themselves, and how they are seen by others.

The following sections discuss the nature of the inward changes experienced by practitioners (*i.e.,* both principals and teachers) in the DL Program, and reveal how practitioner *sensemaking* evolved pre-DL to post-DL. In discussing practitioner perspectives, the following stories reveal how implementing DL, at least as operationalized by the program, can promote transformational learning and second-order change in schools.

Principal Perspectives

For principals at DL schools, creating and supporting teacher leadership in DL schools challenged their notions of who leads, and their role as leaders. Many principals saw themselves as "the one in charge" (Rita, personal interview), and felt it was their role to be both expert and decision-maker. In their framework for leadership, an effective leader was the one responsible for coming up with new ideas and seeing them through. As Susie recounts, "prior to the program I guess [my approach] would be best explained in thinking that I had to do it all, and I had to initiate everything, and I had to ultimately be responsible for everything" (Susie, personal interview, February 20, 2013). The distributed perspective as a framework shifted how principals understood the leadership role, broadening it to include opportunities for teacher leadership and leading to increased collaboration and innovation.

As Rosalie explains, she came to view leadership as "someone who facilitates . . . gets the right people into the right situations to have the best results—that doesn't have to be me." Susie shares a similar perspective, as she began to look to her staff to take on leadership roles in the school:

> What I hooked on to was the idea that as leader, as principal, you can't be the expert on everything, and if you try to be the expert on everything, you're gonna fail. But to look at your staff and to hone in on their expertise and plug into those people to fill in spots that you need to fill in to build a strong school.
>
> (Susie, personal interview, February 20, 2013)

Through the DL Program, principal participants, as a group, widened their notion of leadership to include teacher-leadership roles. Furthermore, these roles were understood as a set of more fluid leadership arrangements that shifted with the demands of a given task, often including both formal teacher leaders and other members of the school community.

The degree of challenge this shift in thinking represented was related both to principals' pre-DL thinking about leadership, as well as to to how they performed their current role. For teacher leaders to take on additional school leadership responsibility, principals had to create space for others to share in the work of leadership. For principals who were already more collaborative, this represented an opportunity to build on the direction in which they were headed and provide a "more formalized structure" for teacher leadership (Rosalie, personal interview). For many principal participants, however, this challenged their understanding of their own role, the way they were perceived in their schools, and their comfort in enacting leadership behaviors that supported teacher leaders in their schools.

Rita is a school principal who struggled with letting go of her authoritarian role in her school. Even though she came to embrace the idea of teacher leadership within a DL model, she found that it displaced her notion of her own role and her relationship to others in her school, particularly in their perception of her as a principal leader. As she explains:

> I feel distributed leadership has definitely totally enhanced, supported, changed, challenged my idea of leadership and being a principal, because I'm still wrangling with the idea that the principal is the one in charge. I'm still wrangling with that, 'cause it's the model that I've seen my whole life, since the time I started school. And also the way you perceive yourself to be versus the way other people perceive you to be.
>
> (Rita, school principal, personal interview,
> February 18, 2013)

Observations and conversations with Rita and teacher leaders at her school reveal an inner tension (a "wrangling") brought on when a new leadership framework (*i.e.*, DL), accompanied by new roles and behaviors for teachers and principals, was introduced in the school. The new system was shifting Rita's understanding of who the leader figures were in her school.

It is of note that not all campuses experienced transformation. Where DL principals experienced transformative change around their support for teacher leaders, it occurred only to the extent to which the system of leader-identity development in their particular schools (see Figure 5.1) and its related parts were able to shift. For example, where a leader's framework was pushed, but their sense of their leadership role remained unchanged, or their leadership behaviors remained grounded in pre-DL models, new ideas tended to chafe against old habits and change was stalled. The ability to embrace new ideas, roles, and behaviors was an indicator of principals' competence and capacity for learning and enacting new leadership behaviors requisite to support teacher-leadership roles. See Chapter 6, Table 6.1.

This shift in leadership behaviors was seen to require principals to not only let go of some areas of leadership authority, but also to actively encourage teacher leaders to step up to the plate. It pushed them beyond what several described as their "comfort zone" with new leadership practices. As Rosalie explains, the DL Project, "forced me to spend more time on curriculum and driving instruction, and really moving outside my own comfort zone in challenging the teachers to kind of boost their level of instruction" (Rosalie, personal interview, July 27, 2011). Principals described how their "confidence level" was a major characteristic in determining how they were able to move forward in their roles.

While the challenge to shift individual leadership practices could hamper the movement towards supporting teacher-leadership roles in DL schools, these changes could also be mutually reinforcing. Principals described that as they were able to shift their thinking, their understanding of their own role, and their leadership practices, this transformation literally gained momentum. Changes in one aspect of the system of their leadership identity and practice supported changes in other aspects, and became part of a movement happening across their schools.

For Susie, the changes she was able to make in supporting teacher leaders became part of a wider shift in leadership thinking and practice across her school. As she was able to make small shifts herself, the enthusiasm and support of other staff members reinforced her behaviors and thinking. She describes how this encouraged teachers and other staff members to understand the sharing of leadership responsibilities across roles in her school:

> If you've empowered other people and you've set this up as this is our style of leadership here, then everyone assumes the responsibility and everyone takes on that responsibility as their own and follows through on it, and it's shared responsibility. But it was hard to do that because it really was a change of my whole idea of leadership, as what I saw leadership as.
>
> (Susie, personal interview, February 20, 2013)

While principals encountered new challenges in working to support teacher leaders at their schools, they also had multiple sources of motivation, which pushed them to encounter and move past these challenges. For example, principals often immediately saw the benefits to instruction by supporting the growth of teacher leadership. Through this structure, teachers were able to share their instructional expertise and encourage more collaboration amongst their staff. Many principals also felt relieved to share responsibility, to not have to do it all:

> My whole understanding of distributed leadership has given me permission not to feel the pressure of having to know it all. So that it's given me the freedom to look for people who can support my limitations.
>
> (Rosalie, personal interview, July 27, 2011)

This sense of relief and the possibility of greater leadership capacity at the school level created the motivation and support that helped principals do the often tough work of shifting their own thinking and practices, as well as the culture of their schools, to support teacher-leadership roles.

The teacher leadership component of the DL Project pushed many principals to experience transformational learning. This occurred as a change in their personal leadership system. The interconnected aspects of their leadership framework, role, and behaviors, along with the broader context of their school, were all implicated in this learning experience. Where deep change occurred, it was not merely an extension of any one aspect; rather, these parts of the system shifted together to support new leadership practices at the school. Transformational learning was seen to involve significant challenge, as new ideas and ways of practicing disrupted past patterns. Principals were motivated by an increasing confidence and a sense of opportunity for positive change at the school level.

While their principals were working to create space for this work, teacher leaders had to take on new responsibilities and develop new relationships with other staff members. Their experiences in doing so presented different challenges from those their principals faced, but the nature and effect of these changes with respect to identity development were quite similar to those discussed above.

Teacher Leaders

Just as principals described how teacher leadership challenged their notion of principals as the ones "in charge," teacher leaders in the DL Project encountered their own conflict between the new expectations of this role and their old thoughts or habits. Across many schools, the creation of teacher-leader roles was experienced to contrast directly with a past culture of teacher isolation and a "teacher mindset" (Andrew, personal interview, February 20, 2013).

Most participants in pre-DL schools described some boundaries around the work of teachers. Teachers tended to focus themselves on the world inside their classroom. One teacher shared:

> [Before the DL Project] the teachers were isolated. They just stayed in their classrooms. They had—whatever was going on in their classrooms, they did that . . . there was really no communication amongst the staff with one another with academic programs here at school. They stayed in their own little worlds, and they did what they needed to do for their grade . . . basically everybody was doing their own thing.
>
> (Ellen, personal interview, January 28, 2013)

This was related both to teachers' individual view of their own work, as well as to the culture of collaboration between teachers. As Drew explains, "my classroom was my world" (personal interview, January 28, 2013).

Stepping into teacher-leadership roles forced teachers to confront a boundary between these past practices and the new leadership responsibilities and opportunities that persisted beyond their classroom walls. While all participants spoke about this difference, they encountered it differently depending upon how they saw themselves as leaders (*i.e.*, their leadership identity), and their support and motivation to push themselves to change. Some teachers saw themselves more naturally as leaders, and this view helped propel them to take on new roles. Others were uncomfortable with the ways these new relationships threatened their understanding of themselves as teachers. In general, the experiences of teacher leaders in the DL Program helped us to understand what it meant for teachers to learn to assume new leadership roles in schools.

The expectation for teacher leadership clashed with many participants' pre-DL understandings of the role of teachers in schools and their sense of themselves in these roles. As one participant explains, "I feel like . . . I'm in no position for anything, 'cause I still just see myself as like a teacher, but I feel like they expect me to know certain things that they don't know" (Andrew, personal interview, February 20, 2013).

The leadership aspect of the new role of teacher leader was seen to clash with certain expectations of teachers for participants, creating a tension for teacher leaders acting in hybrid roles. For Andrew and others, this had to do with how they and peers saw their role. Serving as a teacher leader was seen to create new expectations for their knowledge of and investment in school leadership. They were seen as insiders, privy to something different, by fellow teachers.

This change also threatened perceptions of previous relationships between teachers. Some teacher leaders were uncomfortable with no longer simply being seen as peers with other staff members. They were concerned that the teacher-leader role somehow placed them "above" their colleagues. As Sarah explains:

> I just think of myself more as a teacher than the leader. I don't—maybe it's the title. Maybe like people don't want to be titled. You know what I mean? If you call someone a leader, [rather] than the people coming . . . you know what I mean? I think that we all, in the school, are leaders in our own little sense of in the way, in doing this stuff.
>
> (Sarah, personal interview, January 28, 2013)

Sarah's discomfort with the "title" of teacher leader is related directly to how she sees herself in the role ("more as a teacher"), and how others might see her ("people coming . . ."). Similar to Andrew, she is concerned about other staff members' expectations for or of her. Thus, her framework for leadership is tied to her own leadership role and her school context, creating a boundary for change in her system of leadership. Where such boundaries were shifted by the DL curriculum (see Chapter 3), transformational learning occurred; where they persisted, transformational learning was hindered.

Individual thinking about the isolation of the teacher role was also supported by a culture of isolation at the school level. As one teacher leader explains:

> Teachers are very within their own little world, and if you look beyond that, sometimes it's perceived that, "You need to kind of mind your own business and just worry about what you're doing within your own classroom" kind of mentality.
>
> (Emily, personal interview, February 18, 2013)

Thus, isolation was seen to be reinforced by staff members' collective action and sentiment.

Beyond Teacher Isolation

For teacher leaders, the leadership role was more than just an extension of their classroom teaching. Certainly, the preference was for strong pedagogues to take on teacher-leadership roles, but the learning experiences of teacher leaders drew our attention to the fact that the new demands of the teacher-leader role indicated that a broader system of change was underway (i.e., in respect to leadership identity development, and participatory learning). The movement from teacher to teacher leader was a shift from being an individual, highly autonomous professional to someone responsible for the collaboration and learning of others. This pulled teacher leaders beyond their classroom walls and widened their responsibility, to include how they worked alongside or managed the collaboration of their colleagues. While teacher leaders in the DL Project have no formal supervisory responsibility for other staff, they do become responsible for organizing others to lead instructional change at their schools.

The shift from the individualism and isolation of teaching to the increased responsibility for collective action within a teacher-leadership role posed a challenge for many participants, serving as a key ingredient of teachers' transformative change journey within the DL Project. As participants encountered this boundary between teaching and leading in the role of teacher leadership, many experienced dramatic shifts in their thinking about, and their practice of, leadership at their schools.

Teacher leaders found that this new role contrasted with past practices at their schools. But they also found it pushed them and their relationships with their colleagues. On an individual level, some teacher leaders' obstacles for change were embedded in their confidence and self-image. Furthermore, this was related to teacher-leader enactment of leadership practices. To the extent that teacher leaders became more confident, or tested new tactics, this often supported their shift in thinking and identification.

> Things started to click about the middle of last year. The first couple months were tough. I think for the group I was in, I was never in a leadership role before, so the people who have been here longer were kind of, what, what do you mean? So after, after I was more confident, because in the beginning, I was not, they started to say, oh, okay, she does kind of know what's going on.
>
> (Sharon, personal interview, January 30, 2013)

The above quote reveals how teacher discomfort with a particular leadership framework, roles, and behaviors can block progress and stymie improvement. When teachers personally feel more confident with a new rollout, they tend to project this confidence to others, who in turn impute a relationship between teacher confidence and teacher competence. This underscores how the holistic development of teacher leaders, addressing their personal level of comfort and understanding of a particular rollout, can promote their confidence and project competence to others, enabling transformation within and without a school system.

The Change Process

Studying how teachers came to take on, and principals worked to support, teacher-leadership roles in schools revealed a complex change process.

Rather than merely being painted onto a neutral canvas, new learning was integrated into deeply ingrained habits, ideas, and social relationships. Leaders' frameworks for leadership, leadership roles in their schools (including the social dimensions of these roles), and their leadership behaviors or practices were found to reflect and, together, constitute key aspects of individuals' leader identity (Figure 5.1). These identities further shaped, and were shaped by the particular context of each school community as a site for leadership practice.

Creating teacher-leader roles in schools was seen to impact individual leaders' frameworks, roles, and behaviors. For both teachers and administrators, teacher leadership challenged existing notions of who leads. Collaboration between teacher leaders and administrators further changed the nature of these individuals' roles and relationships to each other. Teacher leaders took on additional leadership responsibility, while principals had to recast their own roles to create space for others to step forward. Furthermore, these changes to roles and relationships required leaders to enact new behaviors. Teacher leaders learned to influence other members of their school community and take responsibility for leadership beyond the walls of their classrooms. Principals shifted from authoritative to facilitative strategies, as they worked to support teacher leaders' efforts to lead instructional improvement in their schools.

For some leaders, the above changes challenged but did not starkly conflict with existing leader identities. Teachers who had always seen themselves as leaders, and principals who had highly collaborative leadership styles, stepped relatively easily into these roles. These participants report being challenged primarily to extend or enhance their past thinking and practices as they worked to embrace teacher leadership at DL schools.

For many participants, however, there existed a stark contrast between the new expectations and demands of teacher-leader roles and deeply ingrained assumptions and practices. This contrast called into question long-held assumptions and working relationships. It pushed participants into new areas of less confident leadership behavior and unfamiliar working relationships with their colleagues. For those who were motivated and supported to persist through these challenges, the change experienced was transformational.

Transformational change did not simply extend participants' leadership practices along existing dimensions. Where and when it occurred, this change remapped leaders' identities. The entire system of this identity—located within the related components of explicit and implicit assumptions about leadership (leadership frameworks), implicating the roles and social relationships between school staff (leadership roles), and enabling and constraining a range of influence practices (leadership behaviors)—was experienced to shift. This change—change in the system of leader identity—was experienced as second-order change.

The implications for how participants learned to take up or support these new roles as teacher leaders lie in how we plan for and support leadership development in schools. Explored more deeply in Chapter 8, this more nuanced understanding of participant learning creates new expectations for how we design the development of leadership capacity.

Rather than simply expecting that teachers will serve in roles as teacher leaders, as an extension of their classroom practice, we must understand how these roles may draw them into new relationships with their colleagues. Learning must be differentiated to account for differences in existing identities across learners. And where we hope for transformational learning to occur, we must plan to have ample support and clear motivation, in order to expect leaders to persist through these changes.

For principals the charge is no less great. Many administrators struggled to understand themselves as capable leaders, while also creating the space for teacher leadership. It led them to question if and when to hold on to formal authority, or to trust in the capabilities of others. It demanded of them new leadership capacity in the form of facilitative and organizational strategies. Support and motivation were also needed for principals to come to take on new roles within the context of teacher-leadership and school-based leadership teams.

Chapter Summary

That transformational learning was such a strong characteristic of the DL Program is a source of great hope. Yet, this type of change was universally experienced as difficult where it did occur. And it did not occur, nor was it found necessary to occur, for all leaders to take on or support new roles as teacher leaders. However, it is exactly this kind of transformation which is the gateway to broader changes in schools.

Changing individual leaders is not enough. But changing, sometimes dramatically, the identity of individual leaders is necessary to lead to the kinds of instructional changes we want to see in schools. In the DL Program, this transformation was a key element in helping schools develop strong teacher leaders and school-based leadership teams, which were the primary vehicles for operationalizing DL and driving instructional improvements. As such, learning to recognize the need for and support transformational learning in teacher leaders and principals is a key component in building the leadership capacity that schools need to improve teaching in ways that will truly transform not only classroom practice, but also student learning.

Chapter Discussion Questions

1. Brainstorm and discuss how professional learning unfolds in your school(s). Then identify whether this learning promotes first-order or second-order change. In terms of building leadership capacity in schools, are there any changes that, if made, could foster transformative learning experiences in your school(s)?

2. Reflect upon how leadership is taught in your schooling context. What do you see as strengths, and what changes would you like to make?

Suggested Reading

- Harris, A. (2003). Teacher leadership as distributed leadership: Heresy, fantasy or possibility? *School Leadership & Management*, *23*(3), 313–324. doi:10.1080/1363243032000112801

- Smylie, M. A., Conley, S., & Marks, H. M. (2005). Exploring new approaches to teacher leadership for school improvement. *Yearbook of the National Society for the Study of Education*, *101*(1), 162–188. doi:10.1111/j.1744-7984.2002.tb00008.x.

- Wahlstrom, K. L., & Louis, K. S. (2008). How teachers experience principal leadership: The roles of professional community, trust,

(continued)

(continued)

efficacy, and shared responsibility. *Educational Administration Quarterly, 44*(4), 458–495. doi:10.1177/0013161X08321502

● York-Barr, J., & Duke, K. (2004). What do we know about teacher leadership? Findings from two decades of scholarship. *Review of Educational Research, 74*(3), 255–316. doi:10.3102/00346543074003255

Note

1. Here "leader" is used to represent both teacher leaders and administrators.

References

Freire, P. (1970). *Pedagogy of the oppressed* (p. 183). New York, NY: Continuum.

Transformative Learning Centre. (2014). About the Transformative Learning Centre. *Ontario Institute for Studies in Education, University of Toronto.* Retrieved July 14, 2015, from: http://tlc.oise.utoronto.ca/About.html

Watzlawick, P., Weakland, J. H., & Fisch, R. (1974). *Change: Principles of problem formation and problem resolution.* New York, NY: W. W. Norton & Company.

Learning to Trust, Learning to Lead

Implications for Leadership Development and Building Relational Trust in Schools

In this chapter . . .

Introduction

The recent attention paid to the role of trust in school improvement (Bryk, 2002) mirrors the identification of trust as a key characteristic of successful teams and organizations in other fields. Trust has been found to improve relationships, facilitate communication and learning, and allow groups to respond quickly and dynamically to changing needs and resources.

Less is known, however, about exactly how trust functions. Leaders are often left with incomplete guidance as to how trust is engendered and what practices support its development at the school level. Implementation of the DL Program sheds new light on both the role trust plays in schools and how trust develops on leadership teams.

As detailed in Chapter 3, several modules addressed aspects of trust on school-based teams and in DL schools as a whole (see Table 3.1, e.g., Module 6: Teamwork and Conflict Resolution; module 7: Building Bridges and Connections; module 12: Collaborative Learning Cultures). Indeed, after several implementations, one modification made to the program was to make the role of trust even more explicit. Program leadership, including the Executive Director and co-author of this book, offered additional training sessions and building-specific coaching, professional development, and support around issues of trust that emerged at specific schools. Also, additional tools were developed for the field, including a trust analysis and formal templates to help school communities form shared commitments in their leadership practices.

The Development of Trust on DL Teams

Trust increased between DL team members and between teacher leaders and administrators across schools, as confirmed by evaluations of the DL Program (see Supovitz & Riggan, 2012). At participating schools, DL teams and teacher-leadership roles proved to be key vehicles for fostering trust. The following themes emerged as supports for nurturing trust in schools through establishing DL teams:

1. Collaborative team space: Participation in DL teams called principals to make space for teachers' voices and ideas in leading school improvement. DL teams offered a formal space for collaboration across administrative and teacher-leadership roles.

2. New roles and norms: DL teams presented structural changes at the school level, shifting traditional roles and norms. Individual teams drove change in their schools through redesigning many formal aspects of their organization, from faculty meetings to professional development cycles.

3. Teacher leadership: DL teams incubated teacher leadership through teacher-led action planning, implementation, and monitoring for continuous school improvement.

The following section presents a vignette followed by a guided reflection that portrays how support for nurturing trust in schools emerges from distributed leadership team activity.

Trust Vignette

Ms. Simone, a math teacher at Wayside Middle School, received the 7th-grade students' performance scores on the state math test. She noted that the 7th-grade population had scored below the state average in math for the past two years. As a member of her school's distributed leadership (DL) team, she suggests to fellow team members that the 7th-grade population receive targeted intervention supports via a one-to-one iPad initiative per each student.

At the DL team meeting, held forty-five minutes before school, Ms. Simone discusses with fellow teacher and administrator team members her idea to offer blended learning supports (i.e., digital media and in-classroom support) to 7th-grade students. Students would pay 50% of the cost of an iPad and the school would fund the rest through grants and support from the central administration office. Ms. Simone proposes several learning apps to be predownloaded on each 7th grader's iPad to offer differentiated, targeted support for each student's individualized learning needs.

Mr. Parker, the science teacher, was thoughtful. Why should the proposed blended-learning approach be limited to math-based intervention? His students had met the state average but barely. And he had ideas about how to use such devices to complement his science classroom's instruction. Mr. Parker mentioned as much to the team, and he volunteered to help work with Ms. Simone on a math/science initiative that would start with the 7th grade before being implemented campus-wide.

(continued)

(continued)

Principal Jones felt relieved. He had distributed students' test scores to teachers earlier that day and, of course, had seen the 7th-grade results. He was scheduled to discuss his school's response strategy with central administration (who were also aware of the scores) later that week. He looks forward to presenting Ms. Simone's initiative as innovative and demonstrative of his school leadership team's resilience in the face of planning for instructional improvement, and he will ask for central administrative grant assistance for the project. Mr. Jones feels confident that Ms. Simone and Mr. Parker, both of whom are well respected by the other faculty and parents, could sell the idea to other teachers, generating buy-in and parental and student support.

In the above vignette, teachers and administrators function as peers, equally committed to guiding school improvement. The Wayside Middle School campus has come a long way. Mr. Jones does not feel the need to solve every problem himself and readily receives Ms. Simone's proposal to incorporate technology in buttressing student learning. Mr. Jones is well positioned as principal to lobby central administration for the resources his campus will need to implement Ms. Simone's action plan. Principal Jones finds that a collaborative leadership team facilitates a shared campus objective (*i.e.*, leading instructional improvement) that does not require the principal to know and do everything himself.

For her part, Ms. Simone, like many teachers in schools, cares whether her students succeed. Offered an opportunity to solve for instructional improvement as a DL team member, she was up to the challenge and proposed an innovative solution.

In the above example, teacher leadership is evident. Rather than being told by the principal what they should do to improve test scores, DL team teachers at Wayside Middle School are comfortable at the helm. Teachers' roles at Wayside have evolved. There is equal opportunity, shared by teachers and administrators, to lead change in the school. For example, Mr. Parker was quick to realize that Ms. Simone would need help in executing her plan, and he was happy to volunteer his time to that end.

His assistance will advance not only the school's math agenda but its science instruction too.

The nature of the interactions between the teacher leaders and principal of Wayside Middle School portray a campus leadership team that shares a common vision and mission, and where all team members feel that they can contribute, and so they do.

But how does the DL team experience in practice facilitate campus culture and leadership transition to that depicted in the Wayside Middle School example? Across schools implementing DL, we asked how and why trust was supported? Knowing *that* trust was supported did not explain *why* trust emerged. Why did teams find specific practices to be effective? What were those practices? And what lessons learned could be shared? To better understand how DL team activity nurtured trust in schools required a clear understanding of, and a framework for, observing trust in schools.

A Framework for Trust in Schools

Obviously, trust is an important resource in school improvement efforts. However, ascertaining *what* trust is may prove difficult for the school administrator or master teacher who knows in their gut when trust is low, yet struggles to identify specific behaviors or practices they can enact to augment trust between the administration and faculty, faculty and parents, or faculty and students. Despite trust's significant role in schools, and the attention that it may receive in school-climate studies and intervention programs, many educational leaders may experience frustration at their inability to design for and/or control so essential a factor in determining a school's success. The answer to this problem lies in part in how we define trust. We cannot design for or control something we cannot identify. And we cannot measure what we cannot see.

Baier (1986) offers a definition of trust as something climatic, observing that, "we inhabit a climate of trust as we inhabit an atmosphere and notice it as we notice air, only when it becomes scarce or polluted" (p. 234). Others have defined trust as a type of "social capital" and resource that accumulates and depletes over time (Fukuyama, 2001) or as admittedly difficult to study or observe because it takes on different meanings in different contexts (Tschannen-Moran & Hoy, 1998). Tschannen-Moran and Hoy

(1998) explain that conceptualizing trust is like "studying a moving target because it changes over the course of a relationship, and . . . can be altered instantaneously with a simple comment, a betrayed confidence, or a decision that violates the sense of care one has expected of another" (p. 335).

Although these descriptions are apt, trust can be hard to pin down if we conceive of it only as something environmental, atmospheric, climatic, cultural, or as an elusive target. And, though available trust theory includes multidisciplinary conceptualizations across organizational science, economics, the behavioral sciences, and philosophy, relatively little attention has been focused "on the nature of trust as a substantive property of the social organization of schools, on how much trust levels actually vary among schools, and how this may relate to their effectiveness" (Bryk & Schneider, 2002, p. 12). The development of the relational trust framework (Bryk & Schneider, 2002) provides a context-sensitive solution in that it both defines and enables the study of trust in schools.

Relational trust is a particular conceptualization of trust as it arises out of interpersonal social exchanges accompanying distinct sets of role relationships in schools: principals with teachers; teachers with other teachers; teachers with students; and teachers with parents. The back and forth that occurs in these social exchanges is better comprehended as a pairing of the expectations of some with the obligations assumed by others; and the *particular intrapersonal meaning(s)* assigned by each party to these exchanges, including interpretations that another party was *respectful*, had *integrity*, was *competent*, and/or was willing to extend themselves beyond their formal role/job definition (*i.e.*, *personal regard*).

One school from the Archdiocesan implementation of the DL Program was selected for a more in-depth case study, based upon the dramatic impact the program had upon trust at this school.

Case from the Field: The St. Ivy DL Team

Prior to implementation of the DL Program, trust at St. Ivy may have been at an all-time low. According to survey results at the beginning of that school year, the St. Ivy DL team had ranked last (*i.e.*, nineteenth out of nineteen participating schools) for teacher perceptions of confidence and trust in the formal school leader.[1] By way of background, St. Ivy began its first year of program implementation during a district-wide teacher strike, pitting teachers directly involved in, or represented by, the union or collective bargaining unit against district administration. This strike, given the hierarchical structure of the Archdiocese, and the significant influence held by the teachers' collective bargaining unit, attested to a rift between administration and teaching body across the Archdiocese. In other words, district-wide, relational trust was low. And at St. Ivy, trust between DL team teachers and campus administration was particularly low.

Based on the teacher strike, the incidence of low trust was hardly surprising. Results from the post-survey, conducted one year after the DL Program implementation, revealed that the St. Ivy DL team had reported an increase of 18.8% in the level of team member trust in the campus principal. This increase in trust was statistically significant (*i.e.*, to a 95% confidence level). The following section discusses the nature of this shift in trust, and the processes through which trust was built across the school.

The St. Ivy DL Team: New Roles, Routines, and Increased Teacher–Administrator Collaboration

At St. Ivy, DL team members internalized a primary tenet of the DL Program's curriculum: the idea that the act of leadership includes all professional activity—to the extent it bears on the core work of the organization—and thus potentially recognizes contribution from everyone. Both teachers and administrators at St. Ivy characterized the cultural changes in the building as a by-product of *teacher awareness,* facilitated by teacher exposure to collaborative, team leadership experiences, and the opportunity to work alongside the administration in new strategic role relationships. To the question, *"As a teacher on the DL team here at St. Ivy, what is your perception of the principal as a leader?"* St. Ivy DL team teachers had the following to say:

> It's evolved over the year. I didn't understand everything that went with James in his role as principal. I picked that up a lot more interacting with him. Outside of a faculty meeting it was never a meeting on a regular basis where we sat with the principal.

I got a greater appreciation for what he does and what he's responsible for and he shared that with us.

(Peter, personal interview, May 24, 2012)

Before I was a member of this team, I don't think I really respected him [campus principal] as a leader, and I think part of it was I don't think I fully understood how much he was dealing with, how many things are on the plate of a high school principal . . . I think what the team has shown me is that he really does have the best interest of the school in mind.

(Paul, personal interview, October 18, 2012)

I think sometimes you point the finger at a different side. You do it because you're ignorant towards what they actually have to do, and this has allowed the barrier to kind of be broken down. I think once that happened, you have five people on the team that are teachers that are very active in the building who communicate and are friendly with many other teachers in the building. When we can genuinely converse with our colleagues and say, "Well, you know, they've got a lot going on," or, "You know what, it really isn't what we thought it was," we were able to break down the misconceptions.

(Mark, personal interview, November 8, 2012)

Before being in the DLT, I didn't know all the implications that— or all the issues that the principals have to work with on a daily basis, because I just had the teacher point of view . . . but I think James is a good leader. He has a lot of character. He has a clear set of beliefs. And he has a vision for our school, and he's not afraid to make decisions based on what would be best for the school, even though some of the decisions may not be as popular.

(Joseph, personal interview, November 28, 2012)

Each teacher on the team communicated the same message: the opportunity to work alongside the principal and interact with him on leadership initiatives led to new understandings of the struggles and challenges which accompany the principal's role.

Before DL, it was logical to ascribe failure to the principal; he had been endowed with greater formal authority, privileges, and responsibility, and was ultimately responsible for instructional success or failure. The reality, however, was that the formal position of principal as leader and manager of the school was blocking teachers from being able to see the person in the role, the task demands that he was under, and the desires and hopes that he authentically held for the school. Whereas before DL it was easy to blame the principal, in working together, it was a signature of the DL team experience to move beyond formal rank, title, or position towards collaboration in and co-ownership of school improvement efforts.

And the teachers were not alone in this sentiment. To the question, *"Looking at the past year, in what areas do you think your leadership team has made the most progress?"* Chris, the assistant principal, said the following:

> I think the most progress is the fact that the trust between the faculty and the administration has grown almost exponentially. I mean there's a lot more trust. I just think *they* [emphasis added] feel, the fact of not just the members of the DLT team, but the members of the faculty . . . I don't know if it's just the fact that our opinion is now getting back to them. I shouldn't say our opinion. More our reasons for doing things are a little more clear to them. So they look at it, it's not an alternative agenda. I mean, there are reasons why we have to do certain things, sometimes even if they're unpopular.
>
> (Chris, personal interview, October 16, 2012)

Above, the assistant principal unambiguously states that the greatest change by the leadership team, in his opinion, was the growth in trust between the teachers and administrators. He further opines that "they feel" (*i.e.*, the teachers) that the administrative team is essentially more trustworthy, an awareness that followed only when teachers were allowed a seat at the planning table. The above quote supports the conclusion that increases in relational trust between administrators and faculty on the DL team primarily followed from perceptual changes among *teachers* on the DL team that shifted teacher-administrator interactions in the school.

Principals' willingness to let go, to share and to co-lead, enabled teacher leaders to learn, direct, and implement team initiatives. The more aware teacher leaders became of the rigors of the administrative job, its burdens and challenges, the more they were willing to assist, co-lead, and negotiate understandings with their peers. And as Mark indicated, once the teachers on the DL team were able to understand the principal's role for themselves, they could then redress misconceptions held by other faculty.

James, St. Ivy's principal, brought more than forty-nine years of administrative experience to his role. Nineteen of those years were at St. Ivy (*i.e.*, nine as an assistant principal, and ten as principal). In discussion, he shared how much he disliked the distance and isolation of the job. Though he had always desired greater collaboration with his teachers, prior principal-led efforts came to no avail. He said, "To have this group assume responsibility, is a relief to me . . . I could have never pulled off this [DL] initiative by myself" (James, field notes, February 21, 2012). In a sense, teacher voices and efforts in the boardroom contributed increased legitimacy and traction to the new leadership impetus. The principal's observation resonated loudly: there really was no "I" in "Team."

This outcome comports with relational trust literature. As discussed above, relational trust is described as arising in relation to and out of the interpersonal social exchanges which give rise to it. These social exchanges take place within dense, complex social networks in schools, and further entail a self-identification process whereby "individuals come to define themselves as connected" to other people within the organization, and/or with the greater organization itself (Bryk & Schneider, 2002, p. 15). Through increased interaction, participants' sense of self is broadened, "developing the 'I' into the 'we,' enhancing the participants' "taste" for collective benefits" (Putnam, 1995, p. 67).

Overall, the DL Program dramatically impacted trust at St. Ivy. A statistically significant shift in trust following the program's implementation had profound implications for other intervention programs seeking to reculture schools in a similar way. And this change had occurred in a high school. All else being equal, leading change in high schools has not had as convincing a record as the many positive accounts of successful elementary school reform (Noguera, 2002). Thus, St. Ivy presented an ideal opportunity for a case study on relational trust in a high school that had implemented DL.

Use of Team Space

At St. Ivy, the seven DL team members used their team meeting space to promote dialogue, collegiality, and for action plan development. At their first meeting, the question was simple: "How do we change the culture in the building?" The DL team decided that the most effective way to shift the school's culture was to take a direct, aggressive approach: the leadership team would codesign and lead a fundamental restructuring of the most salient forum in the school for whole staff, administrator interaction—the faculty meeting. During his interview, Paul, a teacher on the DL team, reflected:

> The first thing we talked about was two Junes ago now when we first started meeting . . . we needed to change the culture in the building and we thought the best vehicle for that change would be changing the way that we do faculty meetings, to make faculty meetings something.
>
> (Paul, personal interview, October 18, 2012)

Across those team members interviewed, the sentiment was the same. The "one focus was to change the culture of our faculty meetings," explained another DL team teacher (Mary, personal interview, October 31, 2012). In restructuring, the DL team decided to convert half the faculty meetings throughout the year into interactive, small-group, professional learning communities, which would gather around teacher-identified topics of interest for in-house, in-service/professional development. The balance of faculty meetings would remain full-staff congregations, led by DL team teachers rather than administrators.

Mary explained that before these changes, teachers were talked to for 45–60 minutes by the administrative team via a pedagogical approach modeled on direct instruction. A senior school official confirmed this, stating that before the DL team changes to faculty assemblies the meetings were boring, never ended on time, and even the administrators found them lacking stimulation and professional interaction. In making the shift, Paul further explained:

> That's how faculties have been doing it for the last sixty years. The principal stands up and says a bunch of stuff and the vice

principal stands up and says more stuff, and then someone else stands up and says some more stuff, and then you go home. We took that notion of "that's the way meetings were" and threw it out the window and said, let's do something different. So what we started to do was, we started to say—we're kind of negotiating with [the principal and assistant principal] at this point and we're sitting in the room . . . telling them and saying, "We understand that you guys need some time to talk but it can't be the entire meeting. It can't even be a large portion of the meeting."

(Paul, personal interview, October 18, 2012)

Dialogue amongst DL team members around shifting the culture in the school had turned to renegotiation of administrator and teacher roles and routines, the apportioning of public airtime, and the repurposing, reorganization, and reorientation of staff meetings.

The case of St. Ivy exemplifies how making space (and time) for team planning and interaction (see Figure 6.1) can be an important step in developing a culture of professional dialogue and respect in a school. Team space, in the form of DL team meetings, was used as a place to identify shared goals and promote a singular identity, mission, and vision. DL Teams were characterized by the following activity:

- Active soliciting of input from team members;
- Active sharing and openness;
- Promoting a singular team identity and vision/mission; DL team as a unit.

Using Bryk's relational trust framework to understand this change more deeply, we see how these behaviors both reflected and promoted a culture of *respect and professional regard* in the schools. An interactive culture of respect and professional regard ("R" in right-hand column of Figure 6.1) was developed as teachers and administrators enjoyed a greater sense of equality in their mutual pursuit of school-improvement initiatives. Leadership practices of collective decision-making, active soliciting of input from team members, and development of a singular team identity were primary ingredients, leading to the successful development of relational trust and a positive school culture.

Across participating schools, as DL teams evolved, the initial culture of openness built through norms of respect and professional regard were reinforced by norms of integrity between team members. On DL teams, team integrity and competence emerged through the following specific behaviors:

- Keeping team member confidence;
- Engaging in focused, purposeful, professional dialogue centered on student learning;
- Using the team meeting space as a *two-way* communicative space.

DL teams that fostered school trust effectively actively used the team meeting space as a two-way communicative space (Figure 6.1). To support the free flow of communication across hierarchy, between teachers and principals, required that team members kept confidences and focused on student learning and professional growth. The development of these focused, collaborative relationships was facilitated by perceptions of

ROLES AND NORMS

• Promoting teachers and administrators as equals	R
• Promoting collegiality and valuing others' opinions	R
• Principal willingness to let go, to share, to colead	C/P

TEAM SPACE   ←→   TEACHER LEADERSHIP

• Active soliciting of input from team members	R
• Active sharing and openness	R
• Promoting a singular team identity, vision/mission; DL team as a unit	R
• Keeping team member confidence	I
• Focused, purposeful professional dialogue centered around student learning	I
• Team meeting space as a two-way communicative space	C/P

• Teacher willingness to promote development of peers/other teachers	I
• Teacher willingness to extend oneself beyond their formal job definitions	C/P
• Teacher willingness to initiate change	C/P

Key: R = Respect; I = Integrity; C/P = Competence/Personal Regard

Figure 6.1 Behavioral Typology: How the DL Program Engenders Trust in DL Teams

Note: Team member interpretations were coded thematically and the following four categories were applied: *respect, integrity, competence,* and *personal regard.* These categories were applied pursuant to the conceptual framework on Relational Trust conceived and developed by Bryk and Schneider (2002).

shared competence and personal regard. It was particularly important for administrators to demonstrate their faith in and reliance upon teacher leaders to accomplish significant leadership tasks. At St. Ivy, this rested in teacher leaders' facilitation of faculty meetings, but across schools this extension of relational trust took other forms, from joint decision-making to teachers leading professional development.

Particular leadership behaviors triggering perceptions across the relational trust framework combined to support the formation and functioning of strong, school-based leadership teams. Figure 6.1 presents a behavioral typology of how the DL Program supported trust development on DL teams by emphasizing particular roles and norms, and the enculturation of teacher leadership at DL schools.

Shifts in Roles and Norms

The task of redesigning faculty meetings was executed by teacher leaders and administrators collaborating to change the requisite school structures and, ultimately, school culture itself. Their efforts to co-lead instructional change shifted leadership roles and norms at St. Ivy.

One year after the faculty meetings were restructured, both DL team members and other school faculty confirmed in interviews that this change was the foremost factor in establishing teacher volition and momentum for other DL team-directed changes, and for leadership influence on campus. Even more telling, when asked about the level of trust between faculty and the DL team, most teachers (unaffiliated with the DL Team) referred to the new-style faculty meeting as the greatest positive change by the team on campus. Members of the greater faculty reported during interviews that this change contributed positively to their trust in DL team leadership as an authentic, new leadership structure. The following interview excerpts of teacher responses to the change include observations from a diverse cross-section of the faculty, including first-year teachers, veteran teachers, male and female instructors, and academic department chairs:

> In terms of the meetings, I definitely think that I get much more out of a faculty meeting now. I walk away with improving somehow as a professional. They still disseminate information, but the

work, the working part of it, usually about forty-five minutes, is definitely a positive part of the faculty meeting.

(Robert, personal interview, November 19, 2012)

As far as observable changes or developments at the faculty meetings, before there would be an agenda, and the agenda could be twenty things. . . . It seems [now] that there's . . . an intention to build in some time for discussion, conversation.

(Gabriel, personal interview, November 30, 2012)

I could see it moving towards trying to give teachers things that they can really bring into their classroom.

(Gwen, personal interview, November 28, 2012)

I like the way that the faculty meetings are run, that instead of having an administrator stand out and just give us a whole lot of information, we [the teachers] are actually contributing.

(Lucy, personal interview, November 28, 2012)

Mary, a DL team teacher confirmed: "I don't hear anybody complaining about the faculty meetings, ever" (personal interview, October 31, 2012). The culture at the faculty meetings had shifted away from a point-by-point administrative business agenda towards facilitating increased professional dialogue among the greater faculty. For a faculty coming off a strike year, having to reckon with a new leadership team structure and other organizational changes with a potential for disruption, this change was pivotal. Though the undertaking to remake faculty meetings was a radical change, it likely owes its successful execution to the fact that teachers helped conceive the idea and were active at the helm and in its implementation and follow-through.

The norms of respect and professional dialogue initially negotiated amongst the DL team were translated to other faculty through newly-arranged staff meetings, complete with new roles, new choices, and leadership routines for *other* faculty. Mark observed that prior to the changes, the administrators were talking *at* teachers for as much as an hour, without interaction or teacher professional exchange. There was talk about professional learning community, but there was no actual practice of the same. There was little room for teacher-inspired creativity, discussion, or innovation. DL team members disrupted this.

Both the collaboration occurring on the DL team itself and the ongoing work to change faculty meetings at St. Ivy shifted established roles and norms for school leaders (Figure 6.1). When teachers were brought to the fore, administrators had to step back and "let go" of control.

The principal's act of letting go made space for teachers' voices and energies in the boardroom, and promoted increased dialogue and sharing of perspective between the two sides. These exchanges contributed to teachers' awareness of the pressures and challenges which shape the administrative role, and powerfully influenced teacher impressions that the principal was *respectful* and *competent*. Across schools, three behavioral norms were found to contribute to trust development:

- Promoting teachers and administrators as equals;
- Promoting collegiality and valuing others' opinions;
- Building principals' willingness to let go, to share, to co-lead.

It is difficult to relinquish or share control, particularly where previously a principal had monopolized leadership influence in his school. Thus, those principal leaders who let go indicated high competence in their role as principal and formal building leader.

The novelty of the DL team structure on campus introduced new roles, routines, and norms for professional personnel. Teachers were more willing to confront *dragging-of-the-feet* behavior with their peers, and principals took on the challenge of letting go of old norms, allowing new norms of co-leadership to develop.

The Role of Teacher Leadership at DL Schools

After learning and implementing new forms of dialogue and respect between faculty and administrators during their team experiences, DL team members moved to model, teach, and share these new norms and practices with the greater faculty. And based on their response, the general faculty was learning that change could be good. Paul explained how the DL team's approach to the greater faculty sought to tap into teachers' passions, their hearts, their reasons for entering the profession, and their overall motivation for the job:

> What DL has done in my mind is that it's kind of empowered the teachers without having to give away any title, without having to give away any salary. It's empowered teachers to take that role, to be willing to express those ideas. We tried doing faculty meetings different ways before distributed leadership. People said, "I just don't want to. Get to the end of the day. I just want to go home. I just want to get out of here. I'll sit in a faculty meeting and grade papers 'cause I'm trying to punch my clock and go home because that's what we've always been used to."
>
> (Paul, personal interview, October 18, 2012)

> What we're trying to do as a team is basically asking that question, "Is that really what you want? You went to all this schooling. Is this really the kind of job where you just punch a clock for forty years and then stop punching a clock?" I don't think so and I don't think that people come into this field thinking that.
>
> (Mark, personal interview, November 8, 2012)

DL team teachers had become advocates for professional growth and were successfully confronting a culture of teacher complacency in their peer-to-peer exchanges. Across schools, teacher leadership was revealed in teachers' willingness:

- To promote development of peers/other teachers;
- To extend themselves beyond their formal job definitions;
- To initiate change.

At St. Ivy, for example, teacher leadership was evident. Teachers questioned faculty during professional meetings and actively sought to inspire one another: Why were the faculty there? Why had they entered the profession? Was the current reality what they had dreamed for themselves? Was this their impact? What if they could do something new that could change things? What would it be? Ironically, the principals initiating a similar line of questioning might have felt abrasive or even

Table 6.1 Descriptive Table of Leadership Behaviors Driving Trust in DL Teams

DL TEAM LEADERSHIP BEHAVIORS

- **Promoting teachers and administrators as equals**
  - Demystifying formal hierarchy.
  - Reinterpreting roles.
  - Share/relinquish power & authority.
- **Promoting collegiality & valuing others' opinions**
  - Collective decision-making.
  - Decisions by consensus.
  - No power plays.
- **Active soliciting of input from team members**
  - Especially principals seeking teacher input.
  - Encouraging teacher/admin dialogue.
- **Active sharing and openness**
  - Active participation.
  - All team members have equal time to be heard.
  - Willingness to share opinions w/out fear.

- **Keeping team member confidence**
  - Not sharing words spoken behind closed doors.
- **Teacher willingness to promote development of peers/other teachers**
  - Willing to tactfully confront *dragging-of-the-feet* behavior with peers.
  - Peer-coaching of other teachers.
- **Focused, purposeful professional dialogue centered around student learning**
  - School organization leverages team member action planning that focuses discourse; non-haphazard conversations.

- **Principal willingness to let go, to share, to co-lead**
  - Sharing decision-making responsibility.
  - Distributing decision-making authority.
  - Co-creating/constructing processes for collaborating with team teachers.
  - Sharing more responsibility.
  - Incubating teacher influence through principal acknowledgement and recognition.
  - Exploiting teacher-held informal power/authority with greater faculty.
  - Alternative use of top-down/bottom-up power/authority.
  - Promoting organic leadership development.
    - Providing space for teachers to volunteer both perspective and energy on the team and in school.
- **Team meeting space as a two-way communicative space**
  - Willingness to share opinions without fear.

Respect/Professional Regard	Integrity	Competence	Personal Regard

• **Promoting a singular team identity and vision/mission; DL team as a unit**
  ○ not *he* or *she*, but *we*.
	○ Through team action planning, teachers have an ownership stake and a formal outlet for teacher influence beyond a professional ethic of care approach and/or their classroom responsibilities.
	○ Collective action planning (e.g., instructional design, planning, etc.) serves as means to involve other faculty members (growth).
		○ Teacher willingness to share disagreement with administrators; administrative response constructive.
		• **Teacher willingness to extend oneself beyond their formal job definitions**
		  ○ Disposition to innovate.
		  ○ Assertive orientation to risk (non-averse); self-directed.
		  ○ Willing to make adjustments in personal routines.
		• **Teacher willingness to initiate change**
		  ○ Teacher action planning helped to promote teacher comfort with promoting shift in the organization.	

RELATIONAL TRUST ELEMENTS

Note: This table presents leadership behaviors, norms, and dispositions that have been found to influence the development of relational trust in schools (Abdul-Jabbar, 2013). The relational trust factors—respect, integrity, competence, personal regard—used in this study are informed by the conceptual framework developed by Bryk and Schneider (2002).

abusive. However, with teachers leading the inquiry for themselves—not as administration puppets but as leaders genuinely interested in professional growth— the discourse incited during faculty meetings inspired participation, teacher buy-in, and co-leadership of school initiatives. In shifting the teacher role from one of passive observer during faculty meetings, to active participant and primary facilitator, a bedrock of relational trust fueled DL team action planning and future reform initiatives at the campus.

Table 6.1 breaks down the types of leadership behaviors driving trust in schools. The behaviors identified represent findings from across schools included in our trust sample, and are sorted into particular facets of relational trust. It presents the same information included in Figure 6.1 but in a format that underscores more effectively the role that specific leadership behaviors can play in promoting particular manifestations of trust in schools.

Knowing how particular leadership behaviors can nurture trust in schools may be pivotal. There is a dearth of research that clarifies how specific leadership activity and ways of being and doing promote relational trust between administrators and teachers. Figure 6.1 and Table 6.1 ably guide practitioners, particularly those in team-leadership and DL environments. See Chapter 8 for suggested tips, tools, and inquiries pertinent to the above.

Chapter Summary

This chapter discusses how relational trust emerged in the DL Program, featuring a case from the field of a high school that implemented the DL Program. It discusses how trust emerged on the DL team in the school, and provides detailed practitioner accounts relating how leadership team members, teachers, and administrators responded to the restructuring resulting from the DL Program implementation. When instituting team-leadership structures and routines, creating a *team space* that facilitated the development of *roles and norms,* which sustained *teacher leadership,* was essential to the development of relational trust in schools. A final table disaggregates the various facets of relational trust, and lists the specific leadership behaviors found to nurture trust in schools.

Chapter Discussion Questions

1. Think about your experiences on teams in the past. How did trust factor in team effectiveness or the lack thereof? What elements of trust (*i.e.*, *respect, integrity, competence, personal regard*) were present? Which were not? Did these elements impact your team's ability to succeed? Why/how?

2. Think about your most positive, successful team experience. Using Table 6.1, what leadership behaviors factored into your team's success? In terms of the behaviors, what could you do, as a leader, to increase trust in your current context?

Suggested Reading

- Bryk, A. S., & Schneider, B. (2002). *Trust in schools: A core resource for school improvement*. New York: Russell Sage Foundation.
- Fukuyama, F. (2001). Social capital, civil society and development. *Third World Quarterly, 22*(1), 7–20.
- Tschannen-Moran, M., & Hoy, W. K. (1998). Trust in schools: A conceptual and empirical analysis. *Journal of Educational Administration, 36*(4), 334–352.

Note

1. These data were collected during an assessment of the Archdiocesan implementation of distributed leadership by the Consortium for Policy and Research in Education (CPRE) including pre- and post-surveys and analysis of DL participant weblogs (see Spillane & Zuberi, 2009).

References

Abdul-Jabbar, M. (2013). *Distributed leadership and relational trust: Bridging two frameworks to identify effective leadership behaviors and practices*. [Doctoral dissertation]. University of Pennsylvania, Philadelphia. Available from ProQuest Dissertations and Theses database (UMI No. 35–62478).

Baier, A. (1986). Trust and antitrust. *Ethics, 96*(2), 231–260.

Bryk, A. S., & Schneider, B. (2002). *Trust in schools: A core resource for school improvement.* New York: Russell Sage Foundation.

Fukuyama, F. (2001). Social capital, civil society and development. *Third World Quarterly, 22*(1), 7–20.

Noguera, P. A. (2002). Beyond size: The challenge of high school reform. *Educational Leadership, 59*(5), 60–63.

Putnam, R. D. (1995). Bowling alone: America's declining social capital. *Journal of Democracy, 6*(1), 65–78.

Spillane, J. P., & Zuberi, A. (2009). Designing and piloting a leadership daily practice log: Using logs to study the practice of leadership. *Educational Administration Quarterly, 45*(3), 375–423.

Supovitz, J., & Riggan, M. (2012). *Building a foundation for school leadership: An evaluation of the Annenberg Distributed Leadership Project, 2006–2010.* Consortium for Policy Research in Education, University of Pennsylvania.

Tschannen-Moran, M., & Hoy, W. K. (1998). Trust in schools: A conceptual and empirical analysis. *Journal of Educational Administration, 36*(4), 334–352.

Part III

Distributed Leadership and Instructional Improvement

Parts I and II attend, respectively, to the use of distributed leadership (DL) as a model for leader development, and the implementation of this model at school sites. In Part III, this work is extended to consider more directly the implications for this work in supporting instructional change and future directions for DL theory and practice. Tips, tools, and strategies for guided reflection are provided to facilitate leadership planning in schools. Part III concludes with a bird's-eye view of the DL Program that presents perspectives on why and how the approach to operationalizing DL in schools, as featured herein, can advance the practice and development of educational leadership.

Building Team and School Leadership Capacity

The Strategies and Routines that Work

In this chapter . . .

Overview of Building Team and School Leadership Capacity

The processes used to build team and school-leadership capacity are different in every school, but draw upon a cluster of strategies. As they progress through the leadership professional development regimen, each team is expected to prioritize school needs (often different from other schools), and each team member is expected to create an action plan, clearly stating their goals, strategies for reaching them, and how progress will be measured. These plans focus the work intensely in each school, while allowing each site to customize improvement planning in a motivational way that engages the building's distributed leadership (DL) team with their professional colleagues and expands leadership networks. Building-based training, strategies, and effective routines support these efforts.

Many strategies and routines developed in the distributed leadership projects build team and school-leadership capacity. School-needs assessments are conducted early in the program for team and building use. Modules featuring professional learning communities and harnessing data analysis and use, are taught early so that teams can design their plans using effective tools and routines. Monthly principal and coach reports are structured to monitor team development and school capacity-building. This chapter describes these processes in detail, offering examples for schools and leaders seeking support in their DL-building process.

Building Effective Teams

Since success is often seeded in the choice of program participants and the development of teams, particular attention should be paid to the selection of schools and team members, a process described earlier in Chapter 2.

In selecting which teachers would serve on their campus DL team, the principal, Project Director and Assistant Project Director reviewed teachers' applications and joined in follow-up interviews with those applicants chosen for their proven leadership qualities and efforts. Reviewers posed questions about prior efforts in leadership within the building. It was our belief that past efforts were more reliable predictors of future success. This belief was confirmed by evaluators, who stated consistently that we "chose the right people." We used the same strategy in choosing leadership coaches.

As discussed in Chapter 3, the instructional design of the program required each school team to attend training sessions together, to facilitate team interaction, develop cohesion, and foster team trust. The instructional design ensured that we simultaneously built personal leadership skills and strong, effective teams. This collaboration in training sessions and leadership team meetings was instrumental in accelerating the development of cohesive teams.

Individual Team Member Action Plans

As teacher leaders and teams gained knowledge, confidence, and skills, each was required to put this expertise to use through the formulation and implementation of an action plan. As Carr and Harris (2001) state in *Succeeding with standards: Linking curriculum, assessment and action planning*, action planning focuses the educational community on measureable goals for excellence (improving student performance) and equity (decreasing gaps among groups of students). We gave team members a structured process to individually identify "high leverage educational activities," and a pathway for delivery, specifying what needs to be done, by whom, and when, as well as evidence of plan effectiveness (see Action Planning Format, Appendix B; see also Chapter 6, discussing a case from the field, and featuring a leadership team action plan to redesign faculty meetings at a participating school).

Action plans were added in year one of the project to crystallize the teams' ideas and to track their progress formally. While the district had improvement and strategic plans, the action plans allowed individual group members and teams to frame individual or group foci for their efforts. The Assistant Project Director conducted the training and revised the plans, while the coaches assisted with implementation. The progress in the action-plan areas proved motivating and substantial, helping us to monitor team members' progress. The prompt of the plan was also instrumental in refocusing teams on their stated goals.

The purposes of the DL Program included not only leader development (*i.e.*, individual capacity building), but also leadership development (*i.e.*, collective capacity building—involving multiple individuals, practices, roles, routines, norms, etc.). Both involved a level of change that was challenging and threatening. This was especially true for second-order change efforts. See Chapters 4 and 5 which discuss *team leadership, change as process, teacher-leader learning*, and *second-order change* in schools.

Developing as a leader, while implementing a productive school action plan, challenges both the individual and their colleagues. It requires that the leader must act with both confidence and motivation while simultaneously learning and reflecting on their efforts. Believing that intrinsic motivation provides the most powerful incentive for such action, and seeing this occur time after time in the field, convinces us that providing practitioners with choice (*i.e.*, the opportunity to choose areas where they feel the greater chance of success and strength) is significant.

For several reasons we believe that choices should be made by individual leaders and teams in determining the focus of individual action plans, and in school-change emphases. For example, assuming their roles as "teacher leaders" empowered teachers to become more active as innovators and collaborators, but this development requires significant social resources, as well as psychological risks. When leaders retain their agency and the ability to choose their leadership focus (as an individual or team), it promises a greater likelihood of success and allows the teacher leader to—with greater psychological safety—transcend their individual comfort zone (see Chapter 5, *transformational learning*). Performing a task or carrying out an action plan where leaders feel supported and experience success is exceptionally important in advancing and developing team member skills as leaders, and their willingness to seize more challenging tasks over time. Freedom of choice was essential for our teachers to move beyond more simple, technical (first-order) changes to more complex, adaptive (second-order) changes that would make a true instructional impact, and build social networks in the school. To this observation, Deci and Flaste (1995) and Daniel Pink (2009) identify choice as a highly motivating condition for adults. We believe this to be especially true with emerging leaders.

In one project an elementary principal described how the flow of a building-level action plan, entitled: *Literacy Achievement through Increased Implementation of Differentiated Instruction, Inclusion, Peer Coaching, Data Analysis and Monitoring,* was developed and implemented. Given as its goal a model of inclusion of special education students, the DL team prepared the staff for changes through professional development and discussions. The principal explains:

> The teacher leaders have initiated "Coffee and Conversation" preschool meetings to share resources. Additionally, the new scheduling, which allows for extended time at grade-level meetings, has increased the focus on data analysis, instructional strategies, and student work. Informal conversations discussing

instruction have been observed on an ongoing basis throughout the building. Staff appear to be much more comfortable sharing their successes, as well as their challenges. The Distributed Leadership Team accomplished everything we had started out to accomplish and more. The team has completed turn-around training for all of the modules we participated in at Penn. They took initiative to do extended research in order to address student and teacher needs. They never turned down a call for assistance or support. They have truly become leaders in our school.

(First project elementary principal)

We believe the principal's testimony above followed from strengths-based leadership. We also believe that affording leaders choice will increase their likelihood of success.

From Leadership and Team Development to Social Networks

Early in their training, teacher leaders are instructed that "the most important function of teacher leaders is to create more teacher leaders." With the support of the coach, leaders developed, implemented, monitored, and assessed individual or group leadership plans throughout their school. This led to the emergence of other leaders within, and increased leadership networks and capacity across the school.

The program design followed the same general pattern and flow in each DL school. First, newly formed leadership teams followed the application process described earlier. Next, team members as a group attended DL training spread across the school year, with several key modules (Distributed Leadership, Professional Learning Communities, Data Analysis and Use, Mission, and Direction) delivered early on. As the teams met, a leadership coach attended meetings and provided guidance and suggestions, but did not direct the meetings. Teams typically met two to four times each month. Together, team members identified instructional needs in their schools and developed action plans to address them. Ann Delehant (2006), in her training on professional learning communities, has suggested this extensive list of possibilities:

- What do your teams do during meeting times?
  - Engage in dialogues about learning.
  - Identify students who need intervention/support/remediation.
  - Identify students who need acceleration.
  - Address barriers to learning.
  - Analyze data to inform planning and instruction.
  - Look at student work.
  - Develop common assessments.
  - Facilitate lesson study.
  - Identify root cause.
  - Develop/modify rubrics.
  - Share units/lessons.
  - Plan interdisciplinary units.
  - Answer the four questions:
    - What do we want all students to learn?
    - How will we know if they have learned it?
    - How will we respond when they haven't learned?
    - How will we meet the needs of those who "already know?"
  - Analyze data to determine professional development priorities.
  - Provide time for teacher learning.

The intended influence of training and coaching on leadership teams can be seen in the Program Logic and Theory of Change structures (see Chapter 2).

Following their participation in training, discussions with fellow team members, and work in leadership team meetings, team members worked individually and sometimes collectively to influence instructional activity in their schools. First, they facilitated routines or participated in group meetings to foster instructional improvement activities. Usually these were at grade level or in subject-matter clusters depending on their expertise. The work of leadership team members here could take at least two forms. Members could either play a leadership role in implementing an action plan they developed with the school leadership team, or they could take a more generic leadership role in helping the groups identify and enact instructional improvement routines, such as reviewing student work, organizing peer visitations, or developing professional learning communities. The generic leadership role could entail encouraging other team members to take on leadership functions in group meetings or in respect to particular tasks. A typical development process was described by an Annenberg elementary principal:

> I am very grateful for the participation in collaborative work at our school by our DL team. They have advised me and supported me as we all work to make this school a better place to work and learn. Our team continues to grow as aspiring school leaders. We have all participated in very meaningful leadership discussions and have shared our views and insights around what is best for our students, staff, and school. I am very impressed that each member has continued with their action plans and has taken Penn DL work seriously. They have taken on additional responsibilities through the years and have been an asset to the school's success. Trust continues to be at its highest level at this time.
>
> We continue to work together in support of student success. Each member has taken on more and more responsibility for the leadership of this school. I have been very pleased that our DL members have become well respected as leaders in the school, as they have taken responsibility in handling many issues that needed an administrative approach. I plan to continue the process of developing new leaders through collaboration and inclusion of diverse thought in the development of our school goals.
>
> I have found that as I continue to allow the school staff to discuss topics and voice their opinions in meeting formats, there is additional buy-in to programs and initiatives in the school. Collaborative approaches make a difference as staff members are allowed to understand reasons for decisions. Regularity in scheduled meetings has been very beneficial to building relationships among all staff members.
>
> (First project elementary principal)

Another way team members could enact leadership in their school was to work with individual teachers. Thus, DL team members either played a leadership role vis-à-vis individual faculty members, or encouraged individual faculty members to take on leadership roles around particular tasks with other faculty members. The training module on peer coaching was added by request to facilitate this process. In this way, team members were building leadership capacity through other faculty members, realizing a key aspect of DL.

The cumulative impact of leadership team members' efforts and the routines established in buildings to enact leadership was a range of strategies, enhanced by other faculty efforts in assuming leadership roles, resulting in a surge of instructional improvement activity in the school. This activity improved instruction, enhanced and changed culture, built capacity, and impacted student achievement. The design and flow of implementation precipitated the achievement of school level and student outcomes identified in the Program Logic and Theory of Change of this Project.

People Support What They Help to Create

People support what they help to create. This is the first generalization that John DeFlaminis taught forty-seven years ago to student government leaders in Massachusetts. He believed it then and we have seen it work now in our work in distributed leadership. The Wallace Foundation discovered that when principals and teachers share leadership, teachers' working relationships are stronger and student achievement is higher (Wahlstrom, Louis, Leithwood, & Anderson, 2010).

Of the many other intended outcomes of the Distributed Leadership Project that are facilitated by sharing leadership, perhaps the most important is building leadership capacity. This does not happen in a vacuum and happens best in vivo (in the work of the DL team or the networks that develop from the teams). Trust and confidence are built in the day-to-day routines of making decisions together and sharing leadership work in the building. The development description of the project is that high trust and greater buy-in result from collaboration and involvement. Confidence builds individual and collective efficacy. Individuals and teams come to believe that they can do it if they try, and they try! When people support what they help to create, they own it and commit to it.

Strategies and Routines that Build Team and School Leadership Capacity

James Spillane mentions that: "A distributed perspective is first and foremost about leadership practice. This practice is framed in a very particular way, as a product of the joint interactions of school leaders, followers, and aspects of their situation such as tools and routines" (Spillane, 2008, p. 11).

Spillane (2008) maintains that:

> In trying to understand the practice of leadership in schools it is critical to attend to organizational routines – one key aspect of the situation. Organizational routines are a taken for granted part of everyday life in organizations. They are everywhere. We need to distinguish here between individual routines and organizational routines. Individual routines include everything from getting up in the morning to getting to work. In contrast, organizational routines involve two or more actors in a "repetitive and recognizable pattern of interdependent actions" (Feldman & Pentland, 2003). From a distributed perspective,

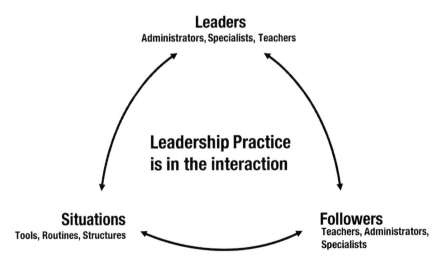

Figure 7.1 Leadership Practice Aspect

Source: Adapted from Spillane, Halverson, & Diamond (2004, p. 11).

aspects of the situation such as tools and routines are an integral constituting element of leadership practice; leaders and followers in interaction with the situation give shape to leadership practice.

(Spillane, 2008, p. 23)

He has underscored the importance of routines (see Table 3.1, Module 2, Unit 4), saying that they shape leadership and management practice, can enable change, and can maintain stability

Further, Spillane (2008, p. 23) has indicated that "organizational routines" include:

1. Grade-level meetings;
2. Faculty meetings;
3. Teacher evaluations;
4. School assemblies;
5. Literacy committee meetings, etc.

In our training, we suggest that an even more comprehensive list would include:

1. Professional learning communities;
2. Teacher collaborations;
3. Data analysis and use;
4. Team meetings;
5. Team action planning;
6. Team ongoing peer coaching;
7. Professional development committees, etc.

These routines are instrumental not only in providing leadership opportunities for teachers, but also in building team and school-leadership capacity (see Chapter 4, *restructuring* and *reculturing* processes in building school-leadership capacity). With every routine successfully undertaken, individual and team confidence grow, and the school's capacity to address significant learning issues is enhanced. Several principals have emphasized this fact in their description of the results of routines, especially of professional learning communities:

> The departments are working effectively as learning communities, sharing ideas within the team. We also have cross-sharing by grade level. We are beginning to notice changes in instructional strategies. I am now receiving questions about different practices and we are seeing more teachers visiting one another. All of this is beginning to lead to improved instruction. And our SAT scores climbed twenty points, we think a good start.
>
> (Second project high-school principal)

Two high-school principals also report a high level of trust with the team, stating that they share ideas openly and honestly. A project one high-school principal shares another compelling example:

> Teachers have formed relationships/learning communities through the collaborative lesson planning groups. The next step for the DLT and our high school is to have teachers and teacher leaders participate in peer walkthroughs to determine the effectiveness of the literacy initiative. These walkthroughs are nonevaluative with teachers providing positive and effective feedback on their visits. Many teachers continue to work together. It was a positive sign when teachers agreed to meet collaboratively without pay. We are encouraged by the open doors of many of our teachers for peer walkthroughs. DLT members were encouraged when other schools commented on our growth and how far we have come as a PLC.
>
> (First project high school principal 1)

One hundred percent of teachers have created a website to communicate with parents and students. Many have opened their door for peer walkthroughs. Teachers have agreed to continue collaborative lesson planning and showed flexibility in finding a resolution. Many teachers continuing to work together, grow together, sharing ideas and strategies, is a good thing. Many conversations continue to be about instruction. We continue to believe that success breeds success, but also know our roles as administrators and instructional leaders can influence adjustments from others.

(First project high school principal 2)

Routines and Professional Collaborations

Cappelletti and Yoak (2014) have written about the role that routines play in understanding the collaborative work of teachers in schools. They have speculated that:

> Routines may be a key component in understanding school leadership from the distributed perspective and provide a framework for us to understand the collaborative work of teachers in schools. Scribner, Sawyer, Watson, and Myers (2007) argue that "improving an organization must take place within, and across, each level of the organization" (p. 96). This tells us that interaction between multiple and diverse organizational actors, or professional collaboration, is critical for organizational improvement. Teacher collaboration serves as a means to distribute leadership to obtain desired professional learning, enhance motivation, and manage change (Scribner, Sawyer, Watson, & Meyers, 2007). As a result, collaboration is essential to developing collective leadership capacity within an organization.
>
> Research on teacher collaboration demonstrates benefits for individual teachers and their teaching practice. Collaboration yields improved teacher efficacy (Shachar & Shmuelevitz, 1997) and more positive attitudes toward teaching (Brownell, Yeager, Rennells, & Riley, 1997) for individual teachers. Individual teachers who work in collaborative environments also report high levels of commitment to teaching all students, high levels of energy and enthusiasm, and high levels of innovation (McLaughlin, 1993, cited in Levine & Marcus, 2010). Additionally, collaboration has implications for practice. Goddard, Goddard, and Tschannen-Moran (2007) argue, "The more teachers collaborate, the more they are able to converse knowledgeably about theories, methods,

and processes of teaching and learning, and thus improve their instruction" (p. 879). As it allows teachers to discuss, analyze, and improve their practice, teacher collaboration may affect teachers' ability to improve student achievement.

(Cappelletti & Yoak, 2014, p. 8)

We should reiterate that the choice of routines is never mandated or directed in this project work. As indicated earlier, choice is paramount and leaders are reminded that they should choose from their strengths, consistent with our beliefs in strengths-based leadership. One of our most effective routines is professional learning communities (PLCs), which has been consistently successful across schools. Cappelletti and Yoak (2013) cite Talbert (2009), who found that "Effective PLCs . . . do not develop and thrive when they are perceived as a mandate for collaboration, as increased pressure to meet benchmarks for student achievement, as unsupportive of their learning needs and improvement efforts, and as creating more paperwork and teacher-evaluation criteria" (p. 563).

Routines and Monitoring Progress

A grounding in distributed leadership is essential to leaders' development; it is one of the earliest modules scheduled. Successive modules focus on both school and organizational needs and teacher-leader needs. Similarly, the PLC module, extensive in strategies and routines, can provide many alternative applications and choices. It is also taught early. Those needs' assessments and audits, conducted to provide perspective for the school teams, make *Evidence-based leadership using data to guide school improvement* a useful early offering, to provide skills as teams and members target action plans to critical school needs. *Mission and direction: Shared vision, values, and commitments* helps to center the teams' focus, and *Developing evidence-based and shared decision-making* adds useful tools as early choices and decisions are made. It is very important to assist leaders (especially principals) to know when and how to involve teacher leaders in decisions, since trust is built early in that process (see Chapter 6 on how principals learn to let go and share leadership roles/activity with teachers).

Regular building visits, as well as coach and principal reports, monitor progress across the teams. The monthly principal reports provide feedback on the team meetings, team dynamics, leadership capacity developments (mission/vision; instructional leadership; PLCs; and professional development), the DL program and coaching progress, and networks and action-plan developments. We also ask about data developments and directions, and personal growth. The coach reports provide similar feedback, but more generally assess team progress. Most important are the insights about the teams' functioning and progress, and any substantial issues with team members or the school. In addition to a requested summary of activities, the following *over-the-last-month* questions are posed:

- How has the DL team been effective in the school?
- How has the DL team grown or developed?
- What have you learned that could improve the team or the school?

Project leaders are prepared to intervene if issues requiring more attention arise.

All reports have been invaluable in monitoring progress and addressing problems quickly. Meetings with principals and coaches occur throughout the year to problem-solve and develop approaches that can support the development of all new leaders in the schools.

Chapter Summary

Team development is an important part of the DL program. Careful choices of program participants and team-building processes are instrumental to success. The development of distributed leadership teams is a predictable and observable process. Strategies and routines that build team member efficacy and team success are important, and are systematically introduced and developed. Routines can foster collaboration and are critical to individual leader development. Choice is an important element of implementation and is guided by team and individual priorities. Progress in development is monitored through the action plans and principal and coach monthly reports, as well as team meeting visits.

Chapter Discussion Questions

1. Evaluate the current leadership structure at your school or district in terms of the framework in Appendix C. What level does your school score on the continuum of leadership? Note: there may be more than one level depending on whether you are analyzing a traditional school, charter school, school district, or otherwise.

2. Is your school using a highly distributed leadership structure? Explain. If not, how might you implement a distributed leadership structure? You may choose to use the action-plan template (see Appendix B), the leadership practice aspect, or another routine or aid to guide your thinking and development.

Suggested Reading

- Bryk, A. S., Sebring, P. B., Allensworth, E., Luppescu, S., & Easton, J. Q. (2010). *Organizing schools for improvement.* Chicago: The University of Chicago Press.
- Deci, E. L., & Flaste, R. (1995) *Why we do what we do: Understanding self-motivation.* New York, NY: Pengiun.
- Dufour, R., Eaker, R., & Dufour, R. (Eds.). (2005). *On common ground: The power of professional learning communities.* Bloomington, IN: National Educational Service.
- Hackman, J. R. (2002). *Leading teams: Setting the stage for great performances.* Boston, MA: Harvard Business School Press.
- Hackman, J. R. (2009). In D. Coutu, Why teams don't work. *Harvard Business Review, 87*(5), 103.
- Louis, K. S., Leithwood, K., Wahlstrom, K. L., & Anderson, S. E. (2010). *Investigating the links to improved student learning: Final report of research findings.* New York, NY: Wallace Foundation.
- Spillane, J. P. (2008). *The distributed perspective: Module two of the distributed leadership series: Diagnosis and design. Facilitator's guide.* Evanston, IL: School of Education and Social Policy, Northwestern University.

References

Brownell, M. T., Yeager, E., Rennells, M. S., & Riley, T. (1997). Teachers working together: What teacher educators and researchers should know. *Teacher Education and Special Education, 20,* 340–359.

Cappelletti, G., & Yoak, E. (2014). *The development and enactment of collaborative professional routines within a context of a distributed leadership intervention.* Washington, DC: University Council of School Administrators.

Carr, F., & Harris, D. E. (2001). *Succeeding with standards: Linking curriculum, assessment and action planning.* Alexandria, VA: Association for Supervision & Curriculum Development.

Deci, E. L., & Flaste, R. (1995) *Why we do what we do: Understanding self-motivation.* New York, NY: Penguin.

Delehant, A. (2006). *Developing professional learning communities. Building distributed leadership in the school district of Philadelphia module: Facilitator's guide.* Penn Center for Educational Leadership, University of Pennsylvania.

Goddard, Y., Goddard, R., & Tschannen-Moran, M. (2007). A theoretical and empirical investigation of teacher collaboration for school improvement and student achievement in public elementary schools. *The Teachers College Record, 109*(4), 877–896.

Levine, T. H., & Marcus, A. S. (2010). How the structure and focus of teachers' collaborative activities facilitate and constrain teacher learning. *Teaching and Teacher Education, 26*(3), 389–398.

McLaughlin, M. W., & Talbert, J. E. (1993). *Contexts that matter for teaching and learning.* San Francisco, CA: Jossey-Bass.

Pink, D. (2009). *Drive: The surprising truth about what motivates us.* New York, NY: Riverhead Books.

Scribner, J. P., Sawyer, R. K., Watson, S. T., & Myers, V. L. (2007). Teacher teams and distributed leadership: A study of group discourse and collaboration. *Educational Administration Quarterly, 43*(1), 67–100.

Shachar, H., & Shmuelevitz, H. (1997). Implementing cooperative learning, teacher collaboration and teachers' sense of efficacy in heterogeneous junior high schools. *Contemporary Educational Psychology, 22*(1), 53–72.

Spillane, J. P. (2008) *The distributed perspective: Module one of the Distributed Leadership series: Leaders, leadership and leadership practice. Facilitator's guide*. Evanston, IL: School of Education and Social Policy, Northwestern University.

Spillane, J. P., Halverson, R., & Diamond, J. (2004) Towards a theory of leadership practice: A distributed perspective. *Journal of Curriculum Studies*, 36(1), 3–34. doi:10.1080/0022027032000106726.

Talbert, J. E. (2009). Professional learning communities at the crossroads: How systems hinder or engender change. In *Second International Handbook of Educational Change* (pp. 555–571). Netherlands: Springer.

Wahlstrom, K. L., Louis, K. S., Leithwood, K., & Anderson, S. E. (2010). *Investigating the links to improved student learning*. University of Minnesota and the University of Toronto: The Wallace Foundation.

Tips and Tools for Building School Leadership Capacity for Instructional Improvement

In this chapter . . .

Introduction

Distributed Leadership (DL), as operationalized through the DL Program, has been demonstrated to positively impact school-leadership capacity. Specifically, the DL Program effectively formed strong leadership teams, developed teacher-leadership capacity, and facilitated instructional improvements at DL schools (Supovitz & Riggan, 2012). Furthermore, leadership capacity has been linked consistently to student learning and school improvement (Robinson, Lloyd, & Rowe, 2008).

In DL schools, leadership teams created a space for teacher leaders and administrators to collaborate on school issues. In particular, teacher leaders were seen to take the lead on instructional issues at the school level, better aligning leadership to the instructional expertise and locus of control for teaching within the building. As teachers first, teacher leaders were able to exercise a range of influence strategies to impact teaching and learning, both within their own classrooms and by serving as coaches, motivators, and resources for other teachers.

Furthermore, the building of bonds between teacher leaders and administrators was a step towards fostering collaboration across the school. These trusting, collegial relationships modeled new norms in DL schools, and were seen to support the ongoing professional learning and motivation of staff across DL schools.

Leadership is a critical mechanism for school improvement because it serves to direct our energies towards instructional improvement. In the DL Program, this was structured explicitly through teacher-leader action plans. DL teams helped schools identify areas for instructional improvement, and mobilize the learning and resources necessary to impact teaching and learning.

For other educational leaders or schools, the question is: "How can the lessons from this program be adapted to your own leadership work or the needs of your school?" The DL Program is but one example of how the distributed perspective may be operationalized in schools. Our hope is that this book and this chapter may serve to draw out some broader lessons learned from this particular implementation.

Leadership *Is* Distributed: Diagnosis

As discussed in Chapter 1, a primary utility of the distributed perspective, as articulated by James Spillane and his collaborators, is as a descriptive lens. From this perspective, DL suggests not that leadership should be distributed but that it already is.

For current and aspiring leaders, one utility of DL theory is to better understand the patterns of leadership distribution in your school, particularly as this may surface some existing assumptions held about exactly who leads, how, and in what contexts. Spillane (2006) divides the distributed perspective into two parts: the Leader Plus Aspect and the Practice Aspect.

The Leader Plus Aspect is often the easiest to conceptualize and is, therefore, both the start and end of many conversations on DL. As Spillane observes: "too frequently, discussions of distributed leadership end prematurely with an acknowledgment that multiple individuals take responsibility for leadership in schools" (Spillane, 2006, p. 3). This has contributed to the tendency for DL to be confused with other theories, including shared, democratic, participatory, and collective leadership (Harris, 2007). The uniting element among these diverse conceptualizations of leadership is their common insistence that multiple individuals, often those without formal authority, can or do lead. The Leader Plus Aspect of the distributed perspective, however, is both a "vital," as well as "insufficient" component in understanding distributed leadership (Spillane, 2006, p. 12).

The Practice Aspect presses us to look beyond simply who leads, and attend to the patterns of interaction among leaders, followers, and the situation. Moreover, these patterns are understood to shift across the demands of particular tasks or responsibilities, forming a constantly unfolding tapestry of actions and interactions. The tools below are designed to help school leaders and others reflect upon the actual or potential distribution of leadership across their communities.

Leader Plus Aspect

While we tend to associate leadership with formal authority, evidence suggests that many people actually influence the core work of schools as organizations. Leaders who are better able to *diagnose* where leadership influence actually exists may then plan more effectively, to acknowledge or align the roles of multiple leaders in the work of school improvement. We also recommend using these tools as ways to surface assumptions across multiple members of the school community. You may be surprised by the variation in where different members of your school perceive leadership influence.

The Practice Aspect

While the Leader Plus Aspect is an important first step towards using the distributed perspective as a diagnostic tool for educational leadership, it is also only part of the picture. The true nature of DL emerges as we attend to patterns

Table 8.1 Leader Plus Analysis Tool

Leadership Function 1: Setting Direction

Who in your school works to help the community identify shared goals?	
Formal Leaders (individuals who are formally assigned responsibility or authority)	**Activities** How do these individuals exert influence (either intended or emergent)?
•	
•	
•	
•	
Informal Leaders (individuals who are influential but without formal designation)	
•	
•	
•	
•	

Leadership Function 2: Developing People

Who in your school influences the knowledge and skills of others, supporting their continual learning and development?	
Formal Leaders (individuals who are formally assigned responsibility or authority)	**Activities** How do these individuals exert influence (either intended or emergent)?
•	
•	
•	
•	
Informal Leaders (individuals who are influential but without formal designation)	
•	
•	
•	
•	

Leadership Function 3: Redesigning the Organization

Who in your school helps establish routines or structures that facilitate effective teaching and learning (meetings, protocols, common practices, etc.)?	
Formal Leaders (individuals who are formally assigned responsibility or authority)	**Activities** How do these individuals exert influence (either intended or emergent)?
•	
•	
•	
•	
Informal Leaders (individuals who are influential but without formal designation)	
•	
•	
•	
•	

of interaction among leaders, followers, and their situation (see Chapter 1). Table 8.1 provides a tool for structured reflection around an identified leadership activity. Engaging with this tool may be productive for formal leaders in their diagnostic and design efforts, but it may also present an opportunity for a school community to surface and challenge the different assumptions we all hold about leadership. By questioning how we understand leadership in our schools, we may reveal opportunities for more effective coordination and collaboration leading to instructional improvement.

Examples of leadership activities:

- Planning professional development;
- Providing feedback to teachers;
- Purchasing books or other materials;
- Selecting educational programs;
- Forming partnerships with outside organizations;

- Communicating with parents;
- Designing school policies (grading, dress code, attendance, etc.);
- Forming teams (inquiry, subject, grade level, etc.);
- Setting instructional goals;
- Determining consequences for student behavior;
- And more . . .

Leadership Practice Reflection Questions:

- Leader(s)
  - Is there alignment between who is leading and the person or persons with (see Table 8.2):
    - Expertise (subject, grade)?
    - Investment (who will be doing the work, representative of what groups, union, grade, subject, cultural or ethnic group)?
    - Resources (time, materials, etc.)?
  - Is there the opportunity for the leadership practice to be strengthened through the addition or deletion of leaders? Should more or

Table 8.2 Leadership Practice Analysis Tool

Leadership Activity What leadership task or responsibility is being carried out? What leadership function does it serve?		
Leader(s) Who is leading? What formal or informal roles do these leaders hold in the school?	**Follower(s)** Who is following? Whose motivation, knowledge, effect, or practice is being impacted?	**Situation** What aspects of the situation are structuring the activity?

fewer people have formal or informal authority for this activity? Who could impact how influence is being exerted?

- Follower(s)
  - What are the expectations of, or demands upon followers? How are they working to actively facilitate the leadership practice? Is this practice engaging all of the necessary followers in order to impact teaching and learning in the school?
- Situation
  - How is the situation structuring the activity? Are there opportunities to strengthen the leadership practice through changes to the situation?
    - Activity focus: Is the agenda or focus of the activity clear? Is time being set aside specifically for this work, or does it need to be?
    - Forms and processes: Are the tools used to structure the activity appropriate to the task? Is it possible that modified tools are being used that have unintended consequences for structuring the activity?
    - Language and bias: Is the language used for communication appropriate for all parties? Are there resources available that would facilitate translation? Is communication culturally proficient, or is there evidence of negative biases about the knowledge or skills of specific groups of people?
    - Time and resources: Are people participating, or being prevented from participating, based upon time and resources? Would participants be more active or engaged earlier or later in the day?

It is difficult to overestimate the importance of the diagnostic lens we take with respect to leadership. How we perceive and understand leadership is structured through our assumptions, biases, and preconceived notions about who leads and how. By surfacing and challenging these mental models for leadership, we open ourselves to new opportunities for increased effectiveness.

In the DL Program, the distributed perspective was considered to be transformational in large part exactly because it shifted how leaders understood leadership as a phenomenon and their own leadership roles.

As leaders came to see these roles differently, they came to embrace new definitions for and boundaries around their leadership practices. And as they understood new opportunities to practice leadership, they grew in their capacity to impact instructional improvement across their schools, as individuals and teams.

However, leadership is not all about diagnosis. It is also about action. As much as we encourage leaders to revisit and understand the diagnostic dimension as a constant part of the reflective cycle of leadership practice, we also appreciate the insistency across the field that leadership theory provides guidance for leadership practice.

The DL Program was designed explicitly to tap into the design dimension of the distributed perspective. As discussed in Chapters 2 and 3, the DL Program operationalized DL theory through multiple components, including teacher-leader roles and leadership teams. While we know not whether every school would or should follow a similar pattern of implementation, the lessons learned from the DL Program nonetheless provide guidance for schools on how to put DL theory into practice.

How Leadership *Should Be* Distributed: Design

The DL Program represents one of the first major operationalizations of DL theory. As such, it provides an opportunity to reflect on how leadership may be distributed purposefully within an organization, attending to the mechanisms for accomplishing this, and asking how and when different patterns of distribution are more appropriate or effective. Rather than insisting that "everyone leads," or that leadership should always be more widely distributed, the DL Program provides training and structures to support school leaders' collaborative efforts to build leadership capacity more effectively in their schools.

Key questions that guide this section include:

- What formal structures can be put in place to impact who leads?
- What roles, like teacher leadership, may be created or enacted to impact the distribution of leadership?
- What is the difference between distribution and delegation?

- In what areas is more focused or more distributed leadership more appropriate?

- How can trust and leadership work together to foster increased coordination and collaboration?

- How may schools increase leadership capacity to impact student learning?

Distributed Leadership Roles: Learning from Teacher Leadership

In the DL Program, many participants experienced the transformational learning that occurred when participants were motivated and supported to move beyond existing boundaries in their thinking and practice. This created an opportunity for second-order change—change not only within the existing system of their leadership practice, but a profound change in the nature of the system of their leadership practice itself.

For leaders looking to implement DL, reasonable questions exist as to the opportunity and need for transformational change at their schools. Would the school benefit from individuals being able to transform their leadership practice? Would teaching and learning improve if groups or teams of teachers were able to change their practices together? As transformational learning involved challenging and then *transgressing* current boundaries, one way to approach this is to review the boundaries that teacher leaders and administrators (principals in particular) encountered in shifting their leadership thinking and practice, in the context of their school-based roles and relationships (see Table 8.3).

Key questions:

- Is second-order change required for individuals or teams to take up distributed leadership in my school?

- How may changes to our existing system of leadership practice benefit teaching and learning?

- What challenges may I expect particular administrators or teacher leaders to encounter in supporting this change?

Table 8.3 Boundary Points Leaders' Systems of Practice

Boundary points for teacher leaders	Boundary points for principals supporting distributed leadership
• Identity as a teacher first. • Relationship to other colleagues. • Culture of isolation between teachers in the school. • Using hard and soft influence strategies.	• Idea of principal as expert and decision-maker. • Desire to be in control. • Movement from authoritative to facilitative leadership strategies. • Trust in leadership capabilities of other members of the school community.

As discussed in Chapter 5, teacher leaders taking on, and principals working to, support new roles as teacher leaders in DL schools challenged individual leaders' notions of who leads. Through looking at how they changed, existing leadership roles, practices, and frameworks were found not to be individual parts which could be easily shifted. Rather, they were found to be linked together by the individual's leadership identity. This identity construct was at the core of leaders' practice and influenced how they thought of themselves and others, as well as the range of influence strategies they practiced at their schools.

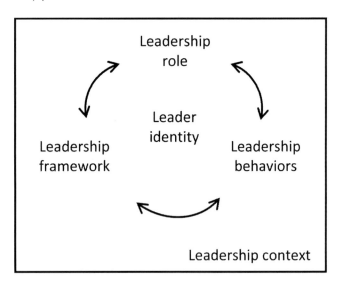

Figure 8.1 Model of Leader Identity in the DL Program

As such, learning to adopt or support new roles as teacher leaders was found to require deep changes to leaders' systems of practice, as grounded by their leader identity (see Figure 8.1; see also Chapter 5). Below, we review some of the specific boundary points individuals encountered, to offer guidance to schools eager to facilitate transformational learning in their schools.

Boundary Points for Teacher Leaders

Many "teacher leaders" in the DL Program were challenged by the very notion of the role. Seeing themselves primarily as a "teacher first," they found that their new role, adding "leadership" to their title, actually diluted or distorted how they thought about themselves. Therefore, they often pushed back against or struggled with the pressure to identify simultaneously, or equally, as teachers and leaders.

The pressure to remain "teachers first" was further supported by existing relationships many teachers held with their colleagues. Some teacher-leader participants had always seen themselves as leaders. For them, there was little challenge in taking on this new relationship to their colleagues. However, teachers who tended to think of themselves on an equal footing with other teachers in their school were challenged by their new roles. They were uncomfortable with other staff looking to them for particular knowledge or advice, or feeling they no longer benefited from the camaraderie they had enjoyed with other members of their school, before they took on additional leadership responsibilities.

These boundaries between the teacher and leader poles of the teacher-leadership role were heightened further in schools with cultures of isolation. Many teachers described how their classrooms were closed off from one another. Teachers operated, and were expected to operate, in isolation from one another. To take responsibility for another teacher's practice, level of collaboration, or shared decision-making was to step over established cultural boundaries at their schools.

Finally, teacher leaders varied in the range of influence practices they enacted in their schools. Many, particularly those identifying first as teachers, enacted soft strategies. They served as resources or mentors for other teachers, or they led by example, either through their classroom practice or by taking on additional responsibilities. However, teacher leaders felt the opportunity and pressure at times to take up harder strategies. Teacher leaders who became comfortable with the leadership end of the continuum reported experiencing success at applying more coercive pressure to their colleagues. Either through direct confrontation or by generating collective pressure, they worked to push other members of their community to improve their instructional practice.

Boundary Points for Principals Supporting Distributed Leadership

Principals encountered difficulty supporting teacher leaders as doing so challenged their notion of their own leadership role as school principals, and pushed them to embrace new leadership practices. Many principals saw their role as that of expert educator and decision-maker. As such, ceding influence over instructional matters and key leadership decisions, either to teams or individual teacher leaders, conflicted with their notion of principal leadership. Some more collaborative principals were well prepared for this change, and it required less transformation of their past thinking and practice. However, many struggled with this change as it displaced their notion of what it meant for them to perform their role well.

Even well-intentioned principals had difficulty letting go, not wanting to abdicate responsibility to their schools. Becoming comfortable with this change required them to find new value in their roles as coordinators or facilitators. Rather than identifying primarily as authoritative experts or decision-makers, they became coordinators or facilitators of others' leadership practices. Furthermore, enacting these new roles required comfort with new leadership strategies, and proved a struggle for many principals. In particular, some established leaders were challenged greatly by new feelings of incompetence as they worked to learn new dimensions of their leadership practices.

Leadership as influence is also deeply related to notions of control. While the distributed perspective presses us to acknowledge our interdependence, and the inherent limitations to our control over the attitudes or behaviors of others, these can be challenging realities for principals to confront in their practice. Being able to choose how and when to step back was tied reciprocally to principals' sense of trust in their teacher leaders. This trust was deepened as opportunities for leadership were extended and teacher leaders stepped successfully into these roles. The initial extension of these opportunities, however, represented significant risk for principal leaders. Regardless of the extension of this opportunity to teacher leaders, principals were keenly aware that responsibility would ultimately be attributed to their leadership for the success or failure of school initiatives headed by teacher leaders or collaborative teams of teachers and administrators.

Planning for leadership learning (reflection questions):

- Who do I expect will learn to enact new leadership practices in my school?
- What boundary points can I anticipate?
- How will I monitor their learning, and the level of support they receive?
- What resources, tools, or strategies can be used to provide a balance of motivation, pressure, and support?

Using Team Structures to Drive School Change

Schools vary widely in their use of teams. At some schools, almost no team structures exist as teachers work largely in isolation, and formal leadership is very hierarchical. At other schools, teams proliferate. Teachers may serve on grade-level or subject-area teams, or teams may be organized around inquiry, Professional Learning Communities (PLCs), or other topics or structures. Some teams may be only teachers, while others may include administration, students, parents, or other members of the school community.

Furthermore, teams may function in a variety of ways. Meetings may occur weekly or monthly. Agendas, facilitation, and outcomes may be clear or ambiguous, well-aligned to the needs of the school or not. And team members' attendance and level of commitment may vary.

The DL Program built strong teams through specific steps and structures. Team members were selected based on nomination and formal interview, conversations with the principal, and program leadership.

Teams participated in intensive leadership training and were supported at their school sites through ongoing coaching. Their members identified specific areas for instructional improvement collaboratively, and constructed action plans individually to impact teaching and learning in their schools.

Strong DL teams shared characteristics across schools. They were defined by norms of trust and collaboration. Teacher leaders played strong roles in leading conversations, particularly around instruction. Administrators respected teacher voice and abided by shared decision-making structures, creating the space for teacher leaders to influence the leadership practices of the school. And through targeted action plans, teams influenced practices across DL schools.

Reflecting on Team Structures

The experience of and research on implementing the DL Program has led to sets of considerations to be taken up by schools looking to implement team structures. A good starting point for any school is to take stock of the current landscape of school-based teams. This poses an opportunity for leaders to reflect on existing structures, considering how these align with their school's needs. Then, leaders may consider which teams, if any, constitute authentic leadership teams.

Table 8.4 Survey of Team Structures at the School Level

School team	Membership (who is on the team and what are their roles?)	Selection (how are team members identified or recruited?)	Leadership tasks and function (what are the team's primary responsibilities?)	Effectiveness (what data do you have on the team's effectiveness?)

Reflection questions:

- Do we need more or fewer teams?
- How are teams aligned to the work of our school, in terms of improving teaching and learning?

Authentic Leadership Teams

Leadership may refer to a wide range of school activities. For example, the definition Spillane (2006) uses encompasses not only effective, but also intended leadership. Furthermore, leadership may be understood to influence organizational members' motivation, knowledge, affect, or practices. This definition purposefully captures a wide range of practices.

Leadership, as defined by Spillane (2006):

> *Leadership* refers to activities tied to the core work of the organization that are designed by organizational members to influence the motivation, knowledge, affect, or practices of other organizational members or that are understood by organizational members as intended to influence their motivation, knowledge, affect, or practices.
>
> (Spillane, 2006, pp. 11–12)

While many schools may have teams, our experience has suggested that few may constitute what we think of as authentic leadership teams (as built through the DL Program). Rather than being imbued with leadership capacity, many school teams simply perform delegated administrative tasks. (For example, Chapter 4 highlights certain differences between DL teams and PLCs.) One of the questions for many schools is if, and how, teams enact leadership.

Given the various ways in which leadership can occur, there may not be one definitive answer as to whether a team exerts leadership influence. In fact, teams may vary from time to time regarding the extent to which they engage in school-wide leadership practices. And those practices may or may not be aligned effectively either with the best interests of the school or with other leadership practices, even introducing the possibility for opposing leadership forces.

Distributed Leadership versus Delegated Leadership on School Teams

In order to help school leaders reflect upon the leadership practices of school teams, we return to the essential questions of influence and the key functions of leadership. Many leaders seek to *distribute* leadership through delegating tasks and responsibilities. What they may often fail to consider is the range of influence available to individuals or teams. What defines leadership teams is their collective capacity to influence their organization's core work. In order to do this, they must be positioned to impact the directional setting, human-capital development, and organizational structuring functions of the school.

In referring to *delegation* we refer to teams with truncated sets of responsibilities. In many such cases, either the team's *ends* or its *means* are constrained by formal administrators, and instructional authority and legitimacy. Table 8.5 outlines key differences between delegated and distributed leadership on school teams.

Table 8.5 Delegated Leadership and Distributed Leadership on School Teams

Delegated Leadership	Distributed Leadership
• School administrators determine the purpose or *ends* of team activities. • Administrators' voices "carry more weight" than those of other team members. • Administrators evaluate and provide feedback to teams on their effectiveness. • Teams have circumscribed spheres of influence: they are expected to function within predetermined boundaries or limits. • Team processes and outcomes are highly controlled from the outset.	• DL teams identify and renegotiate team goals and purposes collaboratively. • All team members' voices are valued equally (though some individuals may be sought out for expertise on particular topics). • Administrators and other team members reflect collaboratively on team effectiveness and mechanisms for improvement. • Teams are expected to have influence where necessary to carry out their work, even if it means focusing or widening the scope of the team's authority or responsibilities. • Team processes and outcomes are emergent and continually renegotiated.

After surveying the teams currently working at your school, you can use the planning tool in Table 8.6 to reflect on which, if any, of these teams constitute Authentic Leadership Teams. As discussed in Chapter 4, key characteristics differentiated DL teams from other team structures at participating schools. These are summarized in Table 8.6, according to the areas of team formation, leadership functions, and building trust.

Table 8.6 Authentic Leadership Team Planning Tool

I. Team Formation

Guiding question: Is the team membership appropriate to the work the team will need to accomplish to be successful?	
Key characteristics	*Evidence/Support*
The team is: • Diverse and cross-functional.[1] • Reflective of different members of your school community. • Responsive to the needs of the tasks for which the team will be responsible. • Comprised of individuals with the expertise to effectively lead the work.	

II. Leadership Functions

Guiding question: Will the team have the institutional authority and resources to impact the core work of teaching and learning?	
Key characteristics	*Evidence/Support*
Direction Setting: • What flexibility or freedom will the team have to identify shared goals? • How will the school legitimize these goals? • Will they be subject to oversight or approval? How will this be negotiated? • How will these goals be expected or permitted to connect to the school's core vision for teaching and learning?	
Human Capital Building: • How will the team develop the capacity of other members of the school to impact teaching and learning? • What resources will be made available?	

Organization Design and Redesign: ● What opportunity will the team have to create or modify existing structures and processes? ● Who else may need to be involved to coordinate these changes?	

III. Building Trust

Guiding question: What leadership practices are in place to develop relational trust across members of DL Teams? (see Table 6.1)	
Key characteristics	*Evidence/Support*
Team Space: ● Active soliciting of input from team members (Respect). ● Active sharing and openness (Respect). ● Promoting a singular team identity and vision/mission; DL team as a unit (Respect). ● Keeping team member confidence (Integrity). ● Focused, purposeful professional dialogue centered around student learning (Integrity). ● Team meeting space as a two-way communicative space (Competence/Personal Regard).	
Roles and Norms: ● Promoting teachers and administrators as equals (Respect). ● Promoting collegiality and valuing others' opinions (Respect). ● Principal willingness to let go, to share, to co-lead (Competence/Personal Regard).	
Teacher Leadership: ● Teacher willingness to promote development of peers/other teachers (Integrity). ● Teacher willingness to extend oneself beyond formal job definitions (Competence/Personal Regard). ● Teacher willingness to initiate change (Competence/Personal Regard).	

[1] Note: DL teams, being both new to most DL schools and focused on improving instructional practices, tended to consist only of teachers and administrators. However, schools should consider if and when to include students, parents, staff, or other members of the school community.

We purposefully move here from the concept of DL teams to the notion of authentic leadership. DL teams, as conceptualized and built within the DL Program, were influenced by multiple program-specific entailments and resources, in terms of how they were constituted and developed. For example, DL teams participated together in extensive professional development and were supported by ongoing coaching. Given that not all schools can access similar resources, the list of authentic leadership characteristics of DL teams seeks to draw out those characteristics which were most crucial to a team's ability to build school-leadership capacity. This is important because it is the leadership capacity for instructional improvement, and not particular elements of the teams themselves, which is the most important driver of student achievement. Thus, authentic leadership teams are, ultimately, those which truly mobilize leadership capacity for school improvement.

The above sections on building trust are also summarized in Chapter 6 (see Figure 8.2). This behavioral typology further demonstrates those relationships between these elements of team trust which were key to developing strong DL teams.

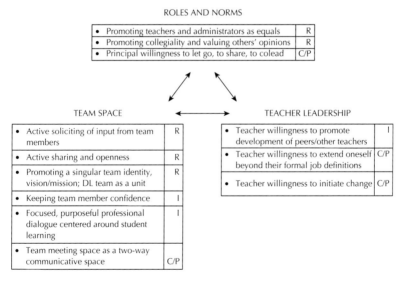

Key: R = Respect; I = Integrity; C/P = Competence/Personal Regard

Figure 8.2 Behavioral Typology: How the DL Program Engenders Trust in DL Teams

Note: Team member interpretations were coded thematically and the following four categories were applied: *respect, integrity, competence,* and *personal regard*. These categories were applied pursuant to the conceptual framework on Relational Trust conceived and developed by Bryk and Schneider (2002).

Chapter Summary

While the DL Program showed positive results for developing school-leadership capacity, not all schools will have the resources to fully implement a similar program. Furthermore, each program implementation of the DL Project was customized for a specific set of schools and district contexts. Similarly, the lessons learned from the DL Project must be adapted to the specific resources and needs of a particular school community.

The above tips and tools should help guide schools and school leaders in implementing DL in their schools. The planning tools and reflection questions can be a starting point for initiating DL. In addition, these resources can provide a helpful structure for evaluating and reflecting upon the successful alignment of leadership practices with the work of improving instruction at your school. Ultimately, evidence demonstrates that schools which continually improve and perform at high levels are those characterized by norms of trust and collaboration, alongside clear instructional goals and strong support systems.

While DL is a valid tool to use in building leadership-capacity schools, our experience demonstrates that effective implementation in schools is not always easy. In order to plan for success, purposeful attention must be paid to the key considerations summarized above, ensuring that leadership activities are aligned to maximize your school community's potential.

Chapter Discussion Questions

1. How is leadership currently distributed at your school? Who do you see in leadership roles? Are some leadership functions more widely shared than others?

2. How will you plan for and monitor the purposeful sharing of leadership? What current arrangements of authority and influence will you need to account for? How will you evaluate the effectiveness of your leadership team(s)?

Suggested Reading

- Spillane, J. P., & Coldren, A. F. (2011). *Diagnosis and design for school improvement: Using a distributed perspective to lead and manage change* (p. 134). New York, NY: Teachers College Press.

References

Harris, A. (2007). Distributed leadership: Conceptual confusion and empirical reticence. *International Journal of Leadership in Education, 10*(3), 315–325. doi:10.1080/13603120701257313

Robinson, V. M. J., Lloyd, C. A., & Rowe, K. J. (2008). The impact of leadership on student outcomes: An analysis of the differential effects of leadership types. *Educational Administration Quarterly, 44*(5), 635–674. doi:10.1177/0013161X08321509

Spillane, J. P. (2006). *Distributed leadership.* San Fransisco, CA: Jossey-Bass.

Supovitz, J. A., & Riggan, M. (2012). *Building a foundation for school leadership: An evaluation of the Annenberg Distributed Leadership Project.* Consortium for Policy Research in Education, University of Pennsylvania.

Revisiting the Distributed Leadership Program

Reflecting on Why/ How it Worked as a Model for Leadership Development

In this chapter . . .

A Comprehensive Leadership Improvement Framework

The Distributed Leadership (DL) Program provided a comprehensive approach to improving organizational leadership capacity in schools, laying the groundwork for new practitioner learning, interaction, and collaboration that disrupted tradition and created space for change.

The program worked primarily through nurturing practitioner understanding and capacity for enacting effective leadership practice. The particular element which ensured the program's success in schools was its emphasis of and impact on developing teacher leadership capacity in participating schools. This feature of the DL Program, further honed by the development of and reliance on collaborative leadership team structures and routines, contributed to effective organizational change in participating schools.

Effective organizational change requires both restructuring and reculturing efforts (Fullan, 2001). Though restructuring efforts can implicate various levels of the leadership hierarchy in schools and districts, including reform efforts promoted conjointly or independently by superintendents, school boards, policymakers, and others, it is *teachers* who have a monopoly over reculturing processes in schools. This is due to their role and proximity to where implementation and execution of action plans occur in schools: the classroom. Regardless of the education reform, its ultimate aim is to impact student learning in classrooms. Thus, the success of any leadership endeavor or improvement initiative in schools rises and falls on teacher-leadership capacity.

The DL Program effects teacher-leadership development through training teachers in *redefining their leadership paradigm* and dispelling the notion that leadership entails formal leadership positions (e.g., the principalship, supervisory posts, and other administrative positions). Teacher awareness that leadership need not follow from a formal role (although it certainly can) but is rather better understood as an activity participated in democratically by all stakeholders, promotes a sense of agency, relieving the burdens of inefficiency that hierarchy imposes on organizational communication and routines.

The DL Program *redefined traditional, rigid relational networks* in participating schools, promoting more dynamic interaction and adaptation by enrolling teacher networks in leadership activity. This was accomplished primarily through teacher participation in DL team structures that: (1) promoted collegial participation and cultivation of norms of respect and professional equality between teachers and administrators; and (2) fostered innovation and overall leadership capacity in participating schools through expanding the definition and density of school leadership networks.

In this way, the DL Program provided a systems-level intervention model for stimulating innovation in practitioner learning and capacity for leading in participating schools.

The DL Program as a Model for Practitioners' Learning and Practice of Educational Leadership

Practitioner learning has been well established as important to implementing school reform (Fullan, 2001; Spillane, 2002). Indeed, the failure of practitioners within the educational system to learn new ways and new approaches is cited as a major stumbling block for educational innovation and improvement (Payne, 2010). But changing traditional notions of leadership in schools and erecting new relational/organizational arrangements is challenging; it may disrupt or threaten long-established systems, norms, and individual beliefs (DeFlaminis, 2011; Evans, 2001). Such disruption may spark resentment or frustration, and seed resistance amongst staff (see Heifetz & Linsky, 2002).

What made the DL Program particularly effective was that the program design relied on team-crafted action planning, where teachers often took the helm. The DL Program change initiatives were crafted, implemented, and executed primarily *by teachers for teachers,* and did not follow from an outside source, imposing solutions on teachers externally. Including teachers in the learning and change process was critical to the program's success, engendering greater buy-in (and necessarily less resistance) among staff.

The DL Program's curriculum was likewise impactful (see Chapter 3). Beforehand, most participants had never thought explicitly or critically about leadership, but the program enabled participant reflection and awareness of members' respective role(s) in leading, and in learning how to lead. Results of the program's implementation revealed that the most evident change was in participants' understanding of and relationship to rigid, constraining, formal hierarchies in their schools. One teacher characterized DL Teams (DLTs) this way:

> DLTs I see more as a force that is able to break away from the current organizational structures, well, that we have here at [our school] . . . So the DLTs tried to break away from that and make it more—to foster that collaboration between departments, between faculty and administration, between the different departments among ourselves, the teaching staff, even between our administration and the principal as well.
>
> (Joseph, personal interview, November 28, 2012)

Again and again, DL participants (administrators and teachers alike) communicated the theme of disruption, change, and being liberated or breaking away from an old mindset.

Distributed Leadership: The New Leadership Paradigm

As explained in previous chapters, distributed leadership theory moves away from the narrative of the "heroic individual as leader" and the view of leadership as only vested in the actions and behaviors of formally recognized individuals (e.g., the principal).

The reality is that school principals cannot be expected to "embody all traits and skills that remedy all the defects of the schools in which they work," or meet all the needs all the time of the students, teachers, families, communities, and the general body of stakeholders who rely on quality schools (Elmore, 2000, p. 14). Alternatively, DL theory supports a reconceptualization of leadership in schools where school leadership responsibility must be and is inherently distributed, taken up, and enacted by all competent, capable teaching and learning professionals in schools. As Elmore (2000, pp. 14f) explains:

> Organizing . . . diverse competencies into a coherent whole requires understanding how individuals vary, how the particular knowledge and skill of one person can be made to complement

that of another, and how the competencies of some can be shared with others.

To this end, the DL Program provided practitioners with explicit training that stressed a reliance on conjoint processes (see Gronn, 2002), and this training took place while members were meeting as teams. Team members worked in and through their teams and benefited from sharing responsibility, expertise, perspectives, and talents. Several school principals indicated psychological and emotional relief that they no longer felt they had to know *everything*, and that they could rely on their teachers to collaborate in shifting school culture, practices, or pedagogy. One school principal related:

> I feel distributed leadership has definitely totally enhanced, supported, changed, challenged my idea of leadership and being a principal, because I'm still wrangling with the idea that the principal is the one in charge. I'm still wrangling with that, 'cause it's the model that I've seen my whole life, since the time I started school. And also the way you perceive yourself to be versus the way other people perceive you to be.
>
> (Rita, school principal, personal interview,
> February 18, 2013)

Another school principal shared a similar thought:

> I see my confidence growing . . . I still think it has a way to go, but I see my confidence building . . . and I feel like I have more tools at my disposal, whether it's research or people, to be able to connect with if I'm not sure, whereas before distributed leadership, I felt limited in that.
>
> (Rosalie, personal interview, July 27, 2011)

DL team member testimony revealed a strong grasp by practitioners of practical strategies for realizing the fruits of DL in their pursuit of continuous school improvement. In promoting practitioner reflection and a burgeoning awareness of the *who*, *what*, and *how* of leadership, the DL Program revealed that learners of leadership progressed through fairly distinct phases of development. See Figure 9.1 for a synopsis of the phases of change observed in leaders' thinking about leadership.

a. Unexamined assumptions about Leadership.	→	b. Surfacing mental models for Leadership.	→	c. Thinking around Leadership theory and practice becomes more explicit and concrete.

Figure 9.1 Changes in Leaders' Thinking about Leadership

Source: Yoak (2013).

Figure 9.1 depicts three distinct phases of practitioner awareness of their thoughts about leadership. Initially, program participants entered the program with largely unexamined assumptions about leadership. Over time, they were able to articulate their personal models for leadership: what they believed constituted leadership practice, and who they felt were positive exemplars of leadership. By the program's end, participants were better able to portray leadership explicitly and concretely, making robust connections among theory, research, and practice. If the goal of the DL Program, and programs like it, includes the ambition of leading change in schools, its results in changing leaders within (*i.e.*, their thinking, awareness, and paradigm), and then enabling them to change the system without, may offer strategic insight. See Chapter 5 for a more detailed accounting of how practitioner learning emerged in the program.

The Black Box of Educational Leadership Practice

Each school year, educators are faced with a challenging, extensive mandate: improve teaching and learning (often measured by standardized test scores); motivate and align the efforts of the teaching staff; generate buy-in with respect to campus initiatives, either recently adopted or already enacted to satisfy state mandates; promote teacher efficacy; promote student efficacy; augment professional capacities in the service of student learning; engage both parents and community in the service of learning; and more. But it is difficult to determine which specific improvement strategies can accomplish these objectives. What exactly works in schools? Confronted with a buffet of options, many school leaders may feel trapped in a cycle of sampling school reform methods, in search of the single best method or cocktail of methods which will produce their desired results. This haphazard approach to leading school change is not effective.

And it may beleaguer those staff called upon to implement one reform one year only to see it replaced by another reform agenda/product the following year. Such frequent reform overhauls may wear on staff motivation as teachers perceive futility in their efforts; no matter the reform initiative, the results continue to disappoint. And this is so because the educational leaders in these circumstances are often unaware of how the inputs of change (*i.e.*, various improvement initiatives) are, in fact, mapping the desired outputs (*e.g.*, school leadership capacity, student achievement, etc.). There is a black box between the inputs and outputs of change that conceals the mechanics of change in schools. See Figure 9.2.[1]

The "black box" contains the policies, practices, and procedures that give rise to the core understanding(s) that surround a given implementation. It contains the action planning, research, practitioner capacities, and activity for any particular implementation. Even where one or more of these elements are known or discussed prior to and/or during an implementation, the breadth and depth of these considerations are rarely shared with those on whose backs a particular initiative will primarily depend during an implementation effort—those who are called on to adapt instructional delivery to the changing needs of students in schools: the teachers.[2]

Thus, while administrators may be familiar with the specific rationale and strategy for realizing a particular teaching-learning objective, teachers rarely understand the *how* themselves. Teachers may not know *how* the initiative is supposed to work, and may be hard-pressed to determine if and to what extent the reform/initiative is working at any given moment. This reality is exacerbated by the fact that data usage in schools, in the context of program implementations, can be applied crudely.

Figure 9.2 The Black Box

For example, poor standardized test scores following an implementation could indicate poor planning, poor process, poor execution, or an ineffective program. But the danger (and even the temptation) exists to attribute failure in its entirety to a program's ineffectiveness. There is little ability to diagnose *how* an implementation effort can best succeed. Though practitioners can readily determine whether an initiative is working or not on the whole, they may be unable to determine what specific routines, practices, and strategies proved effective or ineffective, and how. Thus, unable to determine the *how*, they may be more apt to move from one initiative to the next, accounting poorly for any successes or failures along the way.

With such concerns, the DL Program may prove instructive because it offers a robust accounting of the policies, practices, and procedures that inform teacher-driven, sustainable change in schools. In teaching the distributed perspective to teachers, the DL Program helped school leaders to evaluate educational research and theory more critically as they relate to practice. Practitioners expressed a growing confidence in their ability to design for change via coordination and collaboration with others. And they could better determine how their initiatives were working or not, tailoring their activities accordingly.

We cannot change what we do not understand. And increasingly, those who must readily understand the changes themselves are the teachers who we call upon to implement and execute change in schools. Teaching practitioners how to leverage the distributed perspective can offer a powerful solution to growing leadership capacity in schools. Spillane, Halverson, and Diamond (2004) assert that:

> making the "black box" of school leadership practice more transparent through the generation of rich knowledge about how leaders think and act to change instruction, a distributed perspective can help leaders *identify dimensions of their practice, articulate relations among these dimensions, and think about changing their practice* [emphasis added].
>
> (Spillane et al., 2004, p. 29)

In this way, DL may offer practitioners a means for unveiling the "black box" of educational leadership practice.

Beyond the Black Box of Educational Leadership Practice: Exploring Links among Distributed Leadership, Change, Risk, and Innovation

At the heart of educational leadership is change (*i.e.*, leading change). Change necessarily entails risk. Thus, at the heart of educational leadership is risk. In leading change in schools, educational leaders often must leverage innovative practices, culled from the latest educational research, to overcome practical challenges and barriers to student learning. Though not widely discussed in the educational leadership literature, the relationship between leading change and managing the risk incurred is a staple cautionary tale in business literature (see Heifetz & Linksy, 2002; Kotter, 2012), and in educational policy literature (see Cohen & Moffitt, 2009).

In their work with educational policy, Cohen and Moffitt (2009) describe the nature of the risk inherent in leading change as the risk of *practice failure*—the failure to achieve policy ends due to incompetence, or a lack of capacity which follows from impractical or unreasonable policy objectives. They explain that "the further policies depart from extant practice, the more difficult are the entailed changes in practice, the more incompetence the policy creates, and the more such policies require the acquisition of new capability and the unlearning of existing capability" (Cohen & Moffitt, 2009, p. 23). Thus, the greater the ambition (e.g., student achievement metrics will improve by 50% or higher school-wide), the greater the risk that those called on to realize the ambition will lack the capacity or ability to succeed.

If practice failure results under such circumstances, it is not the fault of teachers but rather of policymakers, who seek to implement action planning

Figure 9.3 The Risk of Practice Failure

and change with no regard for growing and nurturing capacity among the practitioners called on to execute the improvement agenda. To this point, Cohen and Moffitt warn that "the further policy presses practice into the unknown, the more scarce the needed capability becomes, and the more likely is [the risk of] practice failure" (p. 16). Figure 9.3 tracks this risk.

In moving beyond the black box view of educational leadership practice, we encounter the risk of practice failure and incompetence, created by unreasonable expectations (too often accompanied by incomplete supports) imposed on teachers. This risk results from policies requiring leadership capacities not yet in existence, capacities that must be learned, and that are most likely beyond an individual's ability to cultivate alone. But a team leadership design, particularly one supplemented by professional development and team learning, can mitigate the risk of practice failure through distributing risk, ensuring that learning and leading tasks are products of a group process. In this way, DL (as operationalized in the program) distributes risk and leverages group capacity to learn and lead together, enabling practitioners to stretch and grow more effectively towards new leadership skills, competencies, and capacities.

Distributed Leadership as a Disruptive Innovation

Educational innovation has been described as any "new ideas, methodologies, processes, or products that add value and lead to improved outcomes in teaching and learning" (Abdul-Jabbar & Kurshan, 2015). What makes the DL Program *innovative* is the practical novelty of its approach in bringing teacher leadership to the fore, in offering participants a new paradigm of *how* to co-lead across roles and hierarchical assignments in a school. Yet the DL Program was also disruptive. Christensen, Aaron, and Clark (2003) describe *disruptive innovation* as a "powerful force" that "break[s] down the historical tradeoffs between access, cost, and performance" (pp. 21f). They observe that disruption "starts by creating a large, new growth opportunity, almost always by allowing a broader group of people to do things that only experts or the wealthy could do in the past" (p. 20). Thus, disruption starts when participation is democratized beyond the traditionally narrowed niches of practice.

The practice of distributed leadership, as operationalized by the DL Program, is not unlike this description. In teaching practitioners how to use the distributed perspective to guide their own inquiries, data collection, analysis, and action planning, the DL Program facilitated the democratizing of access to the understanding and work of leadership. Beyond administrators, teachers were encouraged to take up the tools and methodologies of leadership practice in their respective schools. In leveraging teacher energies and expanding the base of scholarship and activity such that the traditional, stifling hierarchies in schools were disrupted, the DL Program distributed not only risk, but also the talents and expertise relied upon in nurturing new growth opportunities. The observation that many teaching professionals were launching their own action plan initiatives and action research projects during and after the program comports with Christensen et al.'s description that a broader group of people was now involved in activity that only experts or the principal had done in the past.

Arguably, it is more difficult to teach practitioners *how* to lead rather than merely *what* the best leadership practices are in their field. It is easier to teach practitioners *what* to do and then to hold them accountable (often punitively). Teaching not only administrators but also teachers how to take up a lens for evaluating and reflecting on the leadership practice in their schools invites an intense commitment to leadership preparation, and cannot be achieved quickly. In this regard, "distributed leadership research may prove generative for the field of leadership preparation in that it embraces a conceptual frame that recognizes a greater range of organizational activity as leadership practice" (Yoak & Abdul-Jabbar, 2011, p. 1).

The DL Program offers a model for teaching and training leadership practitioners to draw explicit connections between the theory and practice of educational leadership. Christensen (2013) notes the benefits of teaching explicit connections between theory and practice. Balking at mere data-focused professional development and advocating for leadership instruction informed by theory, he says:

> When we teach people that they should be data-driven and fact-based and analytical . . . in many ways we condemn them to take action when the game is over. The only way you can look into the future—there is no data—[is] to have a good theory . . . . By teaching [leaders] . . . to look through the lens of a theory into the future, [they] can actually see the future very clearly.

Christensen (2013) cautions that a data-driven leadership stance by itself can unwittingly promote delayed, retroactive leadership responses. Teaching theoretical frameworks to leadership practitioners can have the opposite effect: leaders can prepare for the unknown, develop vision, and engage in informed action planning. In our research, we found that teaching educational practitioners to view their enactment of leadership practice through a theoretical lens (*i.e.*, the distributed perspective) contributed greatly to their perceptions of increased personal competence and leadership capacity.

Networked Systems and Distributed Systems of Leadership

Kotter (2012) emphasizes that leadership today requires many change agents to move the organization faster and further in a time of rapid change, and amidst the heightened potential for disruption. However, he advises that this task cannot be accomplished without the adoption of leadership practices that mobilize the oft-unexploited "voluntary energy and brainpower" in the organization (p. 7). He explains further that while traditional, hierarchical systems of management are still necessary, meeting the emerging, requisite demands of systems beset by rapid change requires new leadership operating systems, which offer more distributed networks for developing and sustaining innovative leadership systems.

Though he is primarily addressing a business audience, the circumstances and conditions of rapid change currently distressing the business arena, as described by John Kotter, are remarkably parallel to those likewise affecting the education domain. Educators today are calling for robust leadership systems that offer remedy (if not hiatus) in the face of ostensibly ubiquitous shift and climatic uncertainty, driven and fueled by mounting, high-stakes accountability pressures (e.g., value-added teacher evaluation systems, student standardized testing, and more). Beleaguered educators, despite a flurry of education reforms aimed ultimately at reducing the achievement gap between diverse student subgroups, continue to decry the lack of substantive change and growth in student achievement (see Payne, 2010).

In this regard, DL may provide amelioration if not resolution. The practice of DL is analogous with Kotter's dual-operating leadership system, in that it often manifests programmatically in the leveraging of teacher leaders in schools—mobilizing oft-unexploited, voluntary energies—providing for strategic increase in the overall leadership capacity called on to lead and manage change efforts in educational organizations.

More specifically, the distributed perspective offers a lens for conceptualizing and realizing networked strategic systems of educational leadership that, in the context of our research, have proved equally effective across multiple types of schooling organizations and arrangements. Figure 9.4 presents the DL theory of change observed by the Consortium for Policy Research in Education (CPRE) evaluators during the Annenberg implementation, and confirmed in the Archdiocesan replication of the DL Program.

Figure 9.4 is intriguing because it displays a design similar to that offered by John Kotter in his work on networked systems of leadership in the business arena. This is significant in that Kotter's work, like DL,

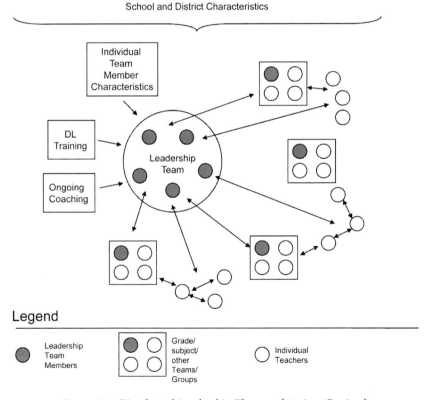

Figure 9.4 Distributed Leadership Theory of Action (Revised)

Source: Adapted from Supovitz & Riggan (2012).

advocates a move away from total reliance on hierarchical systems of leadership (though he does not advocate a complete rejection) in order to ensure that more *efficient* and *accelerative* networked modalities may be leveraged in the name of innovation, creativity, and a host of other positive benefits.

As seen in Figure 9.4, a *distributed* system (similar to what Kotter would call a *networked* system) as designed in the DL Program, leverages teachers' voluntary energies in the organization, and extends or distributes leadership activity and practice throughout a school. In part because of teacher leadership activity, in part because of relational trust, in part because of teaming and robust learning of theory and its recursive connections to practice (*i.e.*, praxis), the DL Program worked to make change possible. Its model confirms the assertion that networked systems of leadership practice can offer school leaders greater efficiency, access to human resources and ingenuity, and greater overall effectiveness in leading school improvement initiatives.

Chapter Summary

As a capstone to preceding chapters, this chapter offers perspective into how and why the Distributed Leadership (DL) Program proved effective in guiding leadership and change efforts in schools. The fact that the DL Program nurtured practitioner learning, interaction, and team collaboration among those called on to implement and execute initiatives (*i.e.*, the teachers) was found to play a pivotal role in the program's success. The particular program element which ensured its success in schools was the emphasis on developing teachers' diagnostic capacity, enabling and informing greater practitioner insight into action planning and leadership activity in participating schools. The program's approach disrupted tradition and created space for change by introducing a *networked* rather than hierarchical leadership structure in schools that distributed risk, and mitigated the likelihood that particular improvement initiatives would fail in practice. The principles shared throughout this book reveal *how* research, policy, and practice, when democratized in schools, can lead to increases in efficiency, access to human resources and ingenuity, and greater overall effectiveness in school improvement planning and execution.

Chapter Discussion Questions

1. How has your understanding of leadership evolved or changed? How might you promote your study as a student of leadership?

2. Knowing that change involves risk, which can lead to "practice failure," how as a leader could you mitigate your team's risk and leverage team capacity? What role would learning and professional development play in your efforts?

Suggested Reading

- Elmore, R. (2000). *Building a new structure for school leadership*. Washington, DC: The Albert Shanker Institute.

- Fullan, M. (2001). *Leading in a culture of change*. San Francisco, CA: Jossey-Bass.

- Heifetz, R. A., & Linsky, M. (2002). *Leadership on the line*. Boston, MA: Harvard Business School Press.

- Kotter, J. (2012). Accelerate: How the most innovative companies capitalize on today's rapid-fire strategic challenges—and still make their numbers. *Harvard Business Review, 90*(11), 1–13.

Notes

1. Although this model implies a linear cause–effect sequence, it is more accurate that there are mediating factors in play, and that an output in one instance can become an input in another. See Day, Gronn, and Salas (2004) describing I-M-O-I (input-mediator-output-input) models.

2. See Heifetz and Linsky (2002) explaining that adaptive leadership requires that those called on to implement change initiatives learn new ways before they can effect desired change. The authors explain that those who are called upon to initiate change (*i.e.*, in schools, our teachers) must be the target population called on to learn adaptive strategies to cope with and advance change.

References

Abdul-Jabbar, M., & Kurshan, B. (2015). Educational ecosystems: A trend in urban educational innovation. *PennGSE Perspectives on Urban Education, 12*(1). Retrieved from http://www.urbanedjournal.org/archive/volume-12-issue-1-spring-2015/educational-ecosystems-trend-urban-educational-innovation.

Christensen, C. M. (2013). Video interview. July 22, 2013. Retrieved from http://www.claytonchristensen.com/key-concepts.

Christensen, C. M., Aaron, S., & Clark, W. (2003). Disruption in education. *Educause*, pp. 19–44.

Cohen, D. K., & Moffitt, S. L. (2009). *The ordeal of equality: Did federal regulation fix the schools?* Cambridge, MA: Harvard University Press.

Day, D., Gronn, P., & Salas, E. (2004). Leadership capacity in teams. *The Leadership Quarterly, 15*, 857–880.

DeFlaminis, J. A. (2011). The design and implementation of the Annenberg Distributed Leadership Project. Paper presented at the annual meeting of the American Educational Research Association, New Orleans, LA.

Elmore, R. (2000). *Building a new structure for school leadership.* Washington, DC: The Albert Shanker Institute.

Evans, R. (2001). *The human side of school change: Reform, resistance, and the real-life problems of innovation.* San Francisco, CA: Jossey-Bass.

Fullan, M. (2001). *Leading in a culture of change.* San Francisco, CA: Jossey-Bass.

Gronn, P. (2002). Distributed leadership as a unit of analysis. *The Leadership Quarterly, 13*(4), 423–451.

Heifetz, R. A., & Linsky, M. (2002). *Leadership on the line.* Boston, MA: Harvard Business School Press.

Kotter, J. (2012). Accelerate: How the most innovative companies capitalize on today's rapid-fire strategic challenges—and still make their numbers. *Harvard Business Review, 90*(11), 1–13.

Payne, C. M. (2010). *So much reform, so little change: The persistence of failure in urban schools.* Cambridge, MA: Harvard Education Press.

Spillane, J. P. (2002). Local theories of teacher change: The pedagogy of district policies and programs. *Teachers College Record, 104*(3), 377–420.

Spillane, J. P., Halverson, R., & Diamond, J. B. (2004). Towards a theory of leadership practice: A distributed perspective. *Journal of Curriculum Studies, 36*(1), 3–34.

Yoak, E. E. (2013). *Learning for leadership: Understanding adult learning to build school leadership capacity.* [Doctoral dissertation]. University of Pennsylvania, Philadelphia. Available from ProQuest Dissertations and Theses database (UMI No. 36–10081).

Yoak, E., & Abdul-Jabbar, M. (2011). A distributed approach to leadership development: How leaders construct conceptual frameworks for practice. Paper presented at University Council for Educational Administration Annual Convention. Pittsburgh, PA.

Conclusion

Implications and Takeaways

The work of leadership development in schools has significant implications for school improvement and reform. When it works, leadership is the driver for building relationships and trust, increasing staff efficacy and motivation, growing school capacity, and realizing student achievement and performance. But figuring out how to get leadership to work, how to operationalize it, can prove difficult.

The perspectives presented in this book reveal lessons learned in the cauldron of the Distributed Leadership (DL) Program, a longitudinal effort that systematically promoted leadership capacity in schools. Lessons learned from this work include the following considerations:

- Team leadership can serve as a useful vehicle for initiating significant change(s) in schools.
- An emphasis on teacher leadership can democratize access to leadership roles, building leadership capacity.
- The distributed perspective can be taught/learned as a new leadership framework, revealing new opportunities and possibilities for leadership practice.
- A focus on *learning to lead* rather than *learning only* or *leading only* can promote leadership development across roles and instructional leadership functions.
- Distributed/networked styles of leading can distribute risk and mitigate the likelihood of practice failure when leading change in schools.

183

- Coaching is an important support for new implementations.

- A new project implementation should focus on how to support and contribute to teaching and learning.

For practitioners seeking either to implement DL in their schools, or just to better understand DL, the above list may be useful.

Leading Improvement Efforts in Schools

The focus of improvement efforts in schools seeks ultimately to promote student learning and growth. From an investment standpoint, it is wise to support the variable in schools that offers the greatest likelihood of realizing schools' core mission: enhancement of teaching and learning. Due to their foremost role in developing students, teachers present the greatest opportunity for schools in leading school improvement, and improvement strategies that invest in teacher leader development can promote efficient resource allocation that directly impacts processes of learning *and* leading in schools. Pulling teachers into the practice of leadership, and developing and teaching them, alongside their administrators and peers, to understand leadership theory, influence, motivation, data, action planning, and staff development—and how such factors relate to leadership practice—can have a powerful effect on school improvement.

The DL Program focused on an approach to building leadership capacity in schools which relied on teacher development and leadership as the catalyst for change and improvement. In focusing on teachers, and grouping them in collaborative team arrangements with their school administrators, expertise and strategic planning were distributed, as were risk and sharing of responsibilities. Teachers became agents of instructional, structural, and cultural change, and entrepreneurship in their own schools, increasing staff buy-in and motivation during the implementation of new initiatives.

The authors hope that practitioners of educational leadership (*i.e.*, traditional and nontraditional, formal and informal, teachers and principals, and others) use this book as a practical tool for guiding reflection on, and planning for, instructional improvement in their schools. To realize this, we have included a complete guide herein: from theory to operation-alization, the program curriculum, analysis and testimony from the field of the effects of the DL Program's approach on practitioner learning, and environmental factors such as trust, plus tips, tools, and takeaways for guiding practitioner reflection. Even where our program, in its entirety, is not a practical solution for your particular program, campus, or district, we hope that lessons learned across project implementations, and shared here, may inform leadership improvement efforts in your school.

Appendices

Teacher Leader Interview Form— Distributed Leadership, 2015

Candidate: _____ School: _____

Date _____

1. Why are you interested in this teacher leader position?

2. In what ways have you demonstrated leadership qualities at this School?

3. Describe a school committee you have been on (i.e. Grade Group, School Council, etc.), and how you contributed to and supported that team.

4. As a teacher leader you will be taking a leadership stance on issues affecting this school. If the team determined that an increase in reading instructional time was needed, and they placed you in charge of implementation, what would you do if some faculty ignored this decision?

5. (a) Since the focus of teacher leaders will be instructional leadership, what are your greatest skills in this domain?

    (b) If we asked a fellow educator to describe your leadership strengths and areas for growth, what would he/she say?

6. What specific skills or talents do you bring to the Distributed Leadership Team?

7. Can you share an experience in which you were a coach or mentor within a school setting?

8. Describe your relationship with the staff in the building, and the extent to which they trust you to look out for their best interests.

9. Do you have any questions of us about this position?

Appendix B
Action Planning Format

The distributed leadership (DL) program provided an action plan template to DL team members to facilitate team planning and development of school improvement initiatives. The action plans became an integral part of the leadership teams' routines and helped to crystallize team knowledge, intent, and their ability to monitor progress.

DISTRIBUTED LEADERSHIP ACTION PLAN

School:	Distributed Leader Member:				Date:	
★	Instructional Improvement Target [or educational practice(s) to be improved]:					

DELIVERY
("How are we going to get there?")
Detail the specific tasks to be completed in order to successfully implement each of the research-based or promising strategies you selected. Complete each column. Use additional sheets, as needed.

Reflect on these high-leverage educational practices . . .	What Needs to Be Done? Specific Actions to Improve Educational Practices (Be sure to identify relevant groups for each item.)	By When? Start/End Dates	By Whom? Persons Involved ('+' denotes lead person)	With What? Resources Required & Funding Source(s)	Evidence of Effectiveness? How will we know our educational practices are working?	DONE?
1. QUALITY TEACHING *1.1 Qualified, effective teacher* *1.2 Rigorous curriculum, reliable assessments, and standards-aligned instructional materials* *1.3 Evidence-based instruction for all, with targeted assistance for "struggling" students, student groups, and staff* **2. QUALITY LEADERSHIP** *2.1 Strong, capable instructional distributed leadership team* *2.2 Unrelenting focus on evidence-based teaching and learning* *2.3 Culture of trust: continuous improvement and accountability for performance* **3. ARTFUL USE OF INFRASTRUCTURE** *3.1 Authentic relationships with staff, families, community, business, and higher education*						

3.2 Strategic alignment and utilization of staff, facilities, time, fiscal resources, and technology				
3.3 Intensive supports for "struggling" districts, schools, and teams				
4. CONTINUOUS LEARNING ETHIC				
4.1 Culture of evidence-based collaborative practice				
4.2 Culture of continuous professional learning				
4.3 Culture of collective professional accountability				

Moving to a Distributed Leadership Structure—A Checklist

Early in the conceptual development of the first project, participants posed many questions about what the development of teams and teacher leaders would look like. A checklist developed in 2006–2007, closely approximating the flow and process of team and leadership development, is included here to guide teams and assist leaders.

Continuum of Leadership Practice

Stage of Implementation	Please Check	Details of Implementation Observed
Level 1 – Traditional Chain of Command		
Level 2 – Leader is Central		
Level 3 – Shared Decision-Making and Authority		
Level 4 – Extensive Shared Decision-Making and Authority		
Level 5 – Distributed Leadership		
Level 6 – Highly Distributed Leadership		

Name _____

Name of School _____   1

Comparing Traditional Leadership & Distributed Leadership

Traditional Leadership	Distributed Leadership
• Information flows through formal and informal channels, based on need to know	• Open and Distributed information system
• Emphasis on stability	• Emphasis on change and adaptability
• Decision-making centers in school leader	• Decision-making shared with team members
• Principal directs the organization's members in influencing the core work	• Direction of organization's members is distributed in influencing the core work
• Emphasis on vertical role structure leadership	• Emphasis on empowered Distributed Leadership

2

Level 1—Traditional Chain of Command

Positions the leader above and separate from the work team.

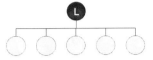

The Leader	Team Members
• Locus of leader command between the team and higher management	• Follow directions. • Work for the leader more so than with each other.
• Has sole authority for decision-making.	• Have limited access to higher management. Provides information to leader as requested.
• Set apart by role, title, and position.	• Limited communication with the leader (mostly around work).
• Directs the organization's members in influencing the core work.	• No direction of organization's members in influencing the core work.

3

Level 2—Leader is Central

Positions the leader from above to the center of the work group (especially for communications) but distinction still exists between what leader and work team does.

The Leader	Team Members
• Leader locus central to team communication and decision-making.	• Rely on leader for information and direction. • Provide information to leader for decision-making as needed.
• Directs most activities.	• Individual leadership may be exercised on non-leader led issues.
• Accessible to all team members.	• Directed by leader on key decisions.
• Directs the team and organization members in influencing the core work	• May affect direction of organization members in influencing the core work.

4

Level 3–Some Shared Decision-Making & Authority

Positions leader central to the team but leader begins to shift decision-making authority. Team members share responsibilities belonging to the leader, who encourages communication, collaboration, and teamwork among team members.

The Leader	Team Members
• Shares decision-making authority in selected areas.	• Involved in decision-making in selected areas.
• Encourages independence/ leadership in selected areas.	• Scope of responsibility expands for some team members.
• Promotes teamwork, collaboration and communication among team members.	• Developing teamwork and collaborative/communication skills.
• Develops team and team members for increased responsibility.	• Growing collaborative team and spirit. May not include entire team.
• Shares direction of organization members in influencing the core work.	• Share some direction of organization members in influencing the core work.

5

Level 4–Extensive Shared Decision-Making & Authority

Leader and team develop confidence in shared decision-making and authority. Team members share more responsibilities belonging to the leader, who encourages even greater communication, collaboration, and teamwork.

The Leader	Team Members
• Shares decision-making authority in more areas and across more team members.	• Involvement in decision-making in more areas and across more team members.
• Encourages independent leadership in more areas and across more team members.	• Scope of responsibility expands for most team members.
• Promotes teamwork, collaboration, and communication among team members	• Strong teamwork and collaborative communication skills.
• Develops interdependent team and team members for increased responsibility.	• Strong, interdependent and collaborative team and spirit.
• Shares direction of organization members in influencing the core work.	• Share more direction of organization members in influencing the core work.

Level 5 – Distributed Leadership

The leader is no longer central to the team and greater interdependence develops and exists between the team members and the leader. The leader has delegated some responsibilities and decisions and the team's authority has increased.

The Leader	Team Members
• Has shifted from sole doer to supporter, coach, and facilitator in distributed areas.	• Assume distributed duties/areas with little assistance from the leader.
• Works with team to expand authority to higher level responsibilities.	• Work closely with school staffs and, in many cases, other team members. Some form their own networks.
• Coordinates the team efforts.	• Assume distributed responsibilities formerly held by the leader and have decision-making authority in those areas.
• Allows others to direct organization members in influencing distributed areas of the core work.	• Direct organization members in influencing distributed areas of the core work.

Level 6 – Highly Distributed Leadership

Team members are self-directed and the leader's role has shifted to other issues, while still providing direction and acting as a resource when needed. Group members are available for more responsibility.

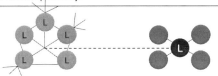

The Leader	Team Members
• Supports, coaches and counsels (as needed) the self-directed teams as they take on increasingly challenging responsibilities.	• Self-directed and confident in distributed leadership areas. Makes decisions in those areas.
• Free to focus on new issues outside the teams.	• Take full ownership of most aspects of delegated areas.
• Identifies new responsibilities for team.	• May be able to assume more new responsibilities. Highly evolved networks develop.
• Delegates to others to direct organization members in influencing distributed areas of the core work.	• Direct organization members in influencing distributed areas of the core work.
• May begin another distributed leadership team in new area.	

8

Index